PRAISE FOR GO

I receive many dozens of books to review each year but I was hooked on Rob Haskell's God of the Mind, quite literally, from page one. Haskell is a great story-teller, has a clear and engaging writing style, and spins the reader, topic by topic, through a tangle of tough issues and questions every thinking Christian—or nonbeliever for that matter—has struggled with. I highly recommend this book to the widest audience, and particularly those whose roots are in the evangelical Christian world.
—Dr. James D. Tabor, retired professor, University of North Carolina at Charlotte

---

"A powerful, personal excavating of the loss of Christian faith. Haskell is the real deal: an informed, thoughtful believer who examined his faith with intellectual integrity and insight and found it deeply problematic. An engaging read for believers and non-believers alike."
—Phil Zuckerman, author of *What It Means to be Moral* and *Society Without God*

Rob Haskell is an "*eXvangelical*" minister who earned two master's degrees in theology. This impressive book showcases the knowledge of an intellectual and the communicative skills of a pastor. Prompted by a crisis in his life his main concern is "how people handle evidence, arrive at conclusions, and make commitments." Just consider how many times in this book he uses the word "question" (110 times) and "evidence" (123 times)!

While he's not adamantly arguing God doesn't exist, he argues "it's difficult to avoid the conclusion that religion is a kind of mind virus." He says, "it seems increasingly possible that God is only a ghost that is flitting around in our brains." When it comes to the claims of religions, he says, "there is almost nothing outside the human mind to suggest any of these claims are factual."

This is an awesome and potentially persuasive book to evangelicals!

—John W. Loftus, author of *Why I Became an Atheist*, and editor of *The Case against Miracles*.

GOD OF THE MIND

AN EXVANGELICAL JOURNEY

ROB HASKELL

APOCRYPHILE
PRESS

Apocryphile Press
PO Box 255
Hannacroix, NY 12087
www.apocryphilepress.com

Copyright © 2024 by Rob Haskell
Printed in the United States of America
ISBN 978-1-958061-71-8 | paper
ISBN 978-1-958061-72-5 | ePub

No part of this book may be reproduced, stored in a retrieval system, or transmitted in any form or by any means electronic, mechanical, photocopy, recording, or otherwise without written permission of the author and publisher, except for brief quotations in printed reviews.

Please join our mailing list at www.apocryphilepress.com/free
We'll keep you up-to-date on all our new releases,
and we'll also send you a FREE BOOK.
Visit us today!

CONTENTS

1. The Great Divorce	1
2. The End Isn't Near	12
3. God's Plan for Your Life	26
4. God's Train Wreck for My Life	35
5. The God Who Doesn't Show Up	45
6. The God Who Doesn't Help	59
7. You Will Burn in Hell for This	69
8. The Messiah Who Doesn't Show Up	88
9. Miracles and Noise	98
10. No Firm Foundation	111
11. Unmasking Conversion	125
12. Conscientious Objector	138
13. Truth with a Capital "T"	156
14. The Post Truth World	175
15. Intellectual Humility	187
Notes	199

CHAPTER 1
THE GREAT DIVORCE

THE ELEVENTH HOUSE

In the days of the Roman Empire, Christians were called atheists because they denied the pagan pantheon of gods and refused to worship them. Christians only believed in one single God. "Imagine that," said the perplexed Romans to each other, "they're a bunch of atheists!"

Modern people are used to hearing attacks on the rationality of Christian belief, starting from the claim that God doesn't even exist in the first place, to arguments about incoherence in the internal logic of Christian doctrine, or the observation that significant swaths of Christian orthodoxy have been rendered highly unlikely by science. Another criticism, one that packs a punch in our current culture wars, is that Christian beliefs lead to unethical attitudes and behaviors. Why are so many Christians so intent on disparaging gays, keeping out poor immigrants, and opposing social justice? It seems like evangelical Christianity in particular is always on the wrong side of conflicts over equality and compassion. Many people are genuinely perplexed and turned off by the set of attitudes that evangelical Christians display in the public sphere.

But while I've been aware of these critiques throughout my life as a Christian, the types of observations that changed *my* mind regarding the truth of Christianity are related to psychology. I don't mean an academic approach based on psychological experiments and PhD dissertations. I am informed by these things to an extent, but I have no formal training in psychology (my training is in theology). What I mean is paying attention to how people, myself included, handle evidence, arrive at conclusions, and make commitments. I've always been drawn to questions about how we think, what forms our opinions, how and why we find some things convincing but others less so, or why it is that two people can look at the same information and come to completely different conclusions. Why is it that we have so many intractable debates that sometimes span centuries, with "smart people on both sides?"

The science of thinking has received a wakeup call in recent years from the study of cognitive biases: our increasing awareness that the human brain is far less objective than we had thought and far more subject to patterned, instinctual responses which often thwart understanding. I found that as I paid more attention to these issues—which I pursued not out of some perverse desire to deny religion or prove people wrong, but rather because I seem to be drawn to them instinctively—I began to see them constantly at play in church, in conversations with my fellow evangelical Christians, from the pulpit, and in public discourse. Not to mention in my own brain. My argument is not so much that Christianity is false, but that it's a colossal misunderstanding, one that arises from the deficiencies of the human mind as it interacts with the world.

Let me explain my point in a parable. John thought his old house was haunted. When asked why, he gave several well-considered reasons. At night he sometimes heard a steady scratching on the windows upstairs, as if someone was trying to get out. But he could not find any physical reason for this noise. There was no tree near the house, and the noise did not seem to be connected consistently to the wind. There was also a swinging door between the kitchen and the living room that scraped when it was opened. John sometimes heard the door scraping in the night, as though in use. He even heard dishes move around, and once a pot clanged loudly on the floor. But when John investigated, he found nothing to explain it. And finally, sometimes at night John was sure that he heard the stairs that go up to his room creaking, as if someone was slowly making their way up them, but trying to do so quietly. John was so concerned about this situation that he had difficulty sleeping, and had on occasion lain in his bed paralyzed with fear, listening to all these sounds and imagining what some ghostly being was doing throughout the house.

It all became too much, and John finally picked up the phone and called in a paranormal investigator to see what could be done about getting rid of his ghost. He needed to get some sleep!

After undertaking an investigation, the paranormal professional had good news: it turned out John's house was not haunted! All the noises that led John to the conclusion that there was a ghost could be explained by natural phenomena. There was no need to draw a supernatural conclusion. The scratching on the window was due to a loose bit of trim that only moved when the wind came from a specific direction. The investigator nailed that back in place so that it would not make any more noise. The swinging door was a bit more complicated. It turned out that John had several stray cats living in his barn, and one of them figured out how to get into the house through a hole in the foundation. From there it went up the basement stairs, through the swinging door, which it learned to push open, and into the kitchen where it rummaged around for food and occasionally knocked over pots. As for the stairs, the investigator explained, "These old staircases creak very badly at night because the wood is contracting with the cold." He recommended that John himself, or a hired professional, use screws to tighten the treads down, and this would take care of most of the creaking.

John was happy. His house was not haunted after all. Everything he feared had a perfectly natural explanation. There was no need to imagine a supernatural being. The ghost, it turned out, was only in his mind, not in the real world. The trim was fixed, and he put a piece of plywood against the foundation to keep the cat out. But he never did anything about the staircase. And even though John now knows that there is a perfectly good non-supernatural explanation for his creaking stairs, there are still some nights when he lays awake listening intently to every little creak and tick of the stairs, wondering if something is coming up them to get him.

Is the world haunted? Does God act in it and do impossible things for our benefit? Or is everything that happens around us, and even within us, explainable as natural phenomena? Could it be that God himself is, like John's ghost, a being who exists only in our minds and only because of a long series of misunderstandings and misinterpretations about how the world works? The paranormal investigator in John's story did not prove that ghosts don't exist. He only proved that there was no supernatural explanation needed in the case of John's house. For all we know there might be other houses which exhibit strange phenomena that are, in those cases, produced by ghosts or demons or monsters. And yet, the more we come across houses that seem to be haunted but are not, the less likely the haunting hypothesis becomes. Ten houses seemed to be haunted but were not. Are we really going to maintain that in the case of the eleventh house there can be no natural explanation? That the eleventh house proves ghosts exist? While this is logically possible and no one can definitively prove there is no truly haunted house anywhere in the world, the haunting of the eleventh house does seem like a bit of a stretch.

But on one level the parable about the haunted house is not a good illustration of belief in God. John does not have anything vested in the idea that his house is haunted. The idea of the ghost just came to him as a result of his experiences. He is relieved, in fact, to find that there is no supernatural being involved. But people who believe in a supernatural religion tend to be extremely motivated to uphold that belief, because it gives them a great deal of meaning. Because of this, those who believe in the supernatural do not call in paranormal experts, so to speak. Instead, they avoid paranormal experts and even denigrate their work and attack their methods. The result is that people who believe in the supernatural are doubly trapped in their view: first, they give superficial impressions, tradition, and circumstances more weight than they are due; second, they cut themselves off from more critical voices that can point out this error.

I can't prove that God does not exist. I don't even want to! I would be glad to find out that such a being created us and is watching over us. But it seems increasingly possible that God is only a ghost that is flitting around in our brains.

ALL MY OLD TRICKS

I remember listening to a radio interview with a philosopher while driving my car on the freeway in Seattle. He was an atheist. He was asked, "What do you think is the greatest challenge to religion?" The philosopher answered, "If I were a religious person, I would be terrified of confirmation bias." For me, this was a moment of revelation, so much so that when I think back on it, I can remember a slice of freeway dividers that I was driving past at the time, like a random photograph that was taken accidentally. Funny how the mind works. That was exactly what I had been thinking, or at least tentatively approaching, but I had not stated it to myself with such clarity.

In those days, whenever I handled evidence related to the truth of Christianity, I was giving far more weight to things which proved my cherished ideas and paying far less attention to the things that challenged them. If all the knowledge available to me could be compared to a book, I would carefully read the parts of that book which supported my views. They would capture my imagination. I would think about them before going to sleep. I would talk about them with my friends. But when it came to the inconvenient parts, I would skim. I would get the gist very quickly and then move on. Or, to be fair, I did sometimes dig deeply into something that made me uncomfortable, but then I would allow myself to forget about it, letting it recede into the background. I remember a couple times thinking to myself, in response to one thing or another which challenged my worldview, "This is just fatal. It's extremely challenging to keep believing in traditional Christianity in the light of this." But then that would somehow fade away, not because I had dealt with it to my satisfaction, but because everything about my mental state, my priorities, and the direction of my life conspired against onboarding that information. The fact that I don't even remember the issues, but only my emotional response to them, is telling. It seems that my ideologically driven brain took a thick black marker to these offensive paragraphs of my book.

I was also adept at compartmentalization. For example, I've always loved science fiction. But that always seemed a bit odd to me given that, with rare exceptions, it is a genre that is unambiguously critical of religion, and which almost invariably paints a future in which religion has been overcome. Sometimes when traveling to teach classes about the Bible I would spend the entire flight immersed in a good sci-fi book. Once, on the way to a theological conference in Atlanta, I read Kurt Vonnegut's *Cat's Cradle*, and I loved it. What was that about? Shouldn't I have been reading the Bible? Or Christian fiction? Or some theology book? In the same way, I was also able to appreciate "heretical" ideas in their own silo, almost as though reading interesting fiction. But I didn't allow those ideas to come to blows with the Christian orthodoxy that lived in the main silo in my head. And if the orthodox and heretical ideas ever passed each other on the street, they were distantly polite to each other.

Don't get me wrong. I did want God to exist, and I did want the whole Christian body of beliefs to be real. And so I came up with some defenses. If God exists, I told myself, then it stands to reason that there will be many things about Him that we would not understand, things which, due to our lack of information or because of our limited reasoning capacity, might seem like contradictions but are not. Since God is not governed by the normal rules of rationality, I would say, we don't need to subject beliefs about him to rationality. But I now see that this is a trick. It is weapons-grade sophistry that allowed me to insert truckloads of incoherence and irrationality into my belief system while all the while thinking I was logical.

Take, for example, something like the virgin birth of Jesus. This doctrine, based on the Bible, claims Mary, the mother of Jesus, did not have sexual intercourse before Jesus was born. Many non-Christians find this hard to accept. On the one hand, it's a biological impossibility. On the other hand, it sounds a lot like a convenient excuse. We are asked to believe that, unlike all the other millions of hot-blooded youths throughout history who had sex before marriage which resulted in an unplanned pregnancy, in this one instance it was a miracle. I find it interesting, and perhaps a little too convenient, that Joseph appears to have died before Jesus began his ministry. If Jesus looked anything like his father, the entire story would have fallen apart.[1] In any case, in quandaries like this one, my reasoning was that if the God of the Bible does exist, there is no problem at all with the idea of miracles, and the virgin birth is really nothing more than a miracle. So, what's the problem? Accept that God exists and all miracles are explained and all irrationalities evaporate. But there *was* a problem. I was defending a miracle by appealing to something which was itself nondefensible and unprovable (the existence of the Christian God). Two unprovables don't add up to proof. The entire strategy was, at bottom, nothing more than the fallacy of assuming that what I was trying to prove was true.

Another one of my coping mechanisms was to appeal to the ideas of struggle, honesty, and mystery. For example, I might have admitted that I was not comfortable with the negative assessment of gay people that comes from both the Bible and evangelical culture. And so, I would occasionally voice this discomfort and then say things like, "This is something I'm struggling with." Or "I'm just being honest." The language of struggle and honesty opens a gray area where an evangelical can express intellectual or emotional discomfort with biblical or theological ideas without following that discomfort through to its logical conclusion. It can also function as a relief valve. Kind of like when you might feel good after discussing your problems with a friend even though that discussion is unlikely to bring about a change in your situation.

Similarly, *mystery* is a very useful concept in which I, like many other evangelicals, have taken intellectual refuge. Mystery can be deployed when something doesn't make sense but admitting it would produce too much cognitive dissonance. A mystery will always be resolved sometime in the future, perhaps even in heaven when all things will be revealed. Issues that for me fell into the area of mystery were:

- If humans can forgive each other without a legalistic blood sacrifice, why can't God do the same? According to the Bible, Jesus had to die on the cross for the sins of the world, or else God would have to send the lot of us to eternal damnation. Why God, who is more loving than all of us put together, can't be bigger than all that is very mysterious.
- If God is managing the whole world and everyone in it, why can't he be a bit more obvious about it? Why can't he be more present? If he could write his name

in the sky occasionally, that would be nice. Or he could make the whole world have a common dream about him. Or what about making the sun blink in Morse code? The options are endless, really. But he stays so hidden that it's easy to confuse hidden with nonexistent. This seems very mysterious indeed.
- Why does the Bible command the destruction of entire cities, including all men, women, and children? Sometimes even the animals. I have enough of an imagination to realize this would be an utter horror show for everyone involved, leaving the victims gruesomely dead and the survivors and perpetrators scarred for life. Additionally, having these sorts of scenes described in a holy book is bound to set a precedent for subsequent readers. The idea that refusing to participate in this sort of massacre could be disobedience to God is mind-bogglingly mysterious.

The appeal to mystery is not an entirely bad thing. After all, my questions do have a host of facile, unconvincing answers from theologians, exegetes, pastors, and weekend keyboard warriors. When someone does not accept those answers, but keeps pondering and eventually lands on mystery, it shows that they are still thinking. In some cases, the mysteries suddenly dissipate—not in heaven, but here on earth—when they draw attention to the fundamental incoherence that caused them in the first place.

DISMANTLING THE SILOS

Back when I was a Christian, I was playing all these mind games while at the same time I considered myself a good evangelical believer. I was working on a thesis for my second master's degree in theology, and I was frequently teaching other Christians how to study the Bible as well. I think I would have kept on doing the same thing indefinitely had it not been for a catastrophic event that woke me from my dogmatic slumbers. I was married, with children. I considered my wife to be an extremely committed Christian, and I was sure that she did not share any of my doubts. She also seemed to be living out the Christian ideals of love and self-sacrifice in an admirable way. All our mutual friends seemed to agree that she was a kind, caring, and exemplary evangelical Christian. But one night, I had a strange dream. I dreamed that I was jealous. This was a new experience for me. I have never been the jealous type, and it never occurred to me that I had anything to worry about. But it turns out I had picked up on something subconsciously, and was trying to tell myself about it. On our twenty-fifth wedding anniversary, we traveled to Vancouver, BC to celebrate. The trip turned out to be terrible. We had no connection, no affection, and she even said things like, "What's in a date? What does it mean anyway?" I thought this was strange and disconcerting. To me, celebrating twenty-five years of marriage meant a lot. When we got home, I retreated to my office to get away from her and the strange vibes she was emanating and to think about what had taken place. After a couple of hours, I landed on the only possible explanation: She must be having an affair. Nothing else made sense.

The next day I found out I was right. In that moment, my whole world came crashing down. In fact, it was worse than an affair. She was unapologetic and gave me a one-two punch: She was in love with this other man, *and* she had never loved me. She said marrying me had been a mistake from day one. In the coming weeks there was a half-hearted attempt to repair the breach in our relationship, but it was doomed. Within a couple of months we had separated, and divorce followed a few months after that. Anyone who has been through this sort of divorce, where there was an affair, knows how intense it can be: the feelings of betrayal, the loss of pride, and just coping with massive change in general. I told a friend that I felt like I had experienced a sudden death in the family.[2]

But once I could come up for some air, I realized something important. The jealous dream I had was a response to the evidence. It was me telling myself that something was very wrong. And as I thought about this and reviewed my memories of the previous years, it dawned on me that the evidence of her dissatisfaction with our marriage was copious. She never wanted to go out and have fun as a couple. She was always tired and clearly arranged her days to avoid time alone with me. She always claimed to be incredibly busy although, in fact, she didn't need to be. And she had also been talking about her male coworkers a lot. In retrospect, it was completely obvious that she was unhappy in our marriage. I even had that specific thought go through my head at one point. I had seen it, and I had understood it. But I had done nothing about it. I had buried that truth, ignored it, and pretended it did not exist while it was staring me straight in the face. I was paralyzed because I did not know how to approach the problem; I just didn't want to deal with such a difficult situation; and this had all happened so gradually that I had acclimated to it without realizing it. To this day I wonder how things might have gone if I had faced the facts and done something about it.

The realization that I could ignore and bury something so important, and the catastrophic consequences that arose from that, led me to a "never again" decision. I promised myself that I would not play these games anymore, that I would pursue questions and doubts no matter how uncomfortable they made me, and that I would live a more authentic life of the mind.

CHAPTER 2
THE END ISN'T NEAR

Once I dreamed that it was the end of the world. We were all standing around looking up at the sky. Jesus was about to come down, and all would finally be revealed. I felt a sense of expectation, and I was painting pictures in my mind about what it might all look like. But there was something else too, which soon came to the surface: In truth, I didn't really think it was going to happen. I didn't really think the skies were going to crack open and reveal the Son of God, descending in supernatural majesty among billowing clouds and shafts of light. It was like when you really want something to work out—getting the best job ever, or your crush falling in love with you—things which are totally out of your control and you really want to happen, but you are keenly aware on some level that the expectation is unreasonable.

That's what I felt.

As much as I wanted this to be real, I was pretty sure it just wasn't. The skies weren't going to part and Jesus wasn't going to come down. And in the dream, he didn't. Nothing happened. At the time I had the dream I was still a Bible teacher, fully engaged in a Christian ministry I had started, and I found it disquieting. It was the rumble of a distant earthquake in my psyche. Things were shifting down there somewhere, apparently without any conscious input from me. I realize now that I was adjusting to a new perception of reality.

The more I thought about it, the more unlikely the expectation of Jesus' return seemed. But all my evangelical friends and family members believed it unquestioningly. I've since asked myself: How is this expectation of a global supernatural event that once and for all deals with all the problems of the world, and conveniently rewards long-suffering believers, different from the ends of the world predicted by many fringe religious movements and cults?

PREDICTIVE FAILS

In the mid-19th century William Miller, a Baptist minister in Vermont, gained prominence for his prediction that Jesus would return on December 31, 1843. The date came and went with no discernable return, so he recalibrated for March 21 of the next year. Finally, after yet another no-show, Miller landed on October 22, 1844. And as we all know by now, Jesus did indeed come back in supernatural glory for all to see, and it was the end of the world. Oh wait, that isn't quite right! What happened was nothing. Just like in my dream. This final date was aptly named "The Great Disappointment," and after it many people rightly abandoned Miller and his teachings. But a committed core did not give up and began promoting the idea that something important had indeed happened on the final date. It was less physical (or shall we say less real?) than expected, to be sure. But nevertheless, the faithful Millerites claimed that some sort of spiritual or heavenly event had occurred in October of 1844, and this belief is still part of the teachings of Seventh-day Adventists, an active Christian denomination. When people want to believe something badly enough, they will always find an explanation, no matter how unlikely or suspiciously self-serving.

Another fringe Christian group, the Jehovah's Witnesses, also tried their hand at predicting the return of Jesus. Starting in 1874, they forecasted his return five times over a period of 100 years. When the first prediction failed to materialize, they concluded that Jesus had returned invisibly and that he was gathering followers with a view to a "real" return in 1878. When that date came and went with no metaphysical intrusion, there followed another prediction for 1881. With each failed prediction a new spiritual explanation, an event that would take place out of the view of prying physical eyes, was put forward to save the day. The next date was 1914, and when this did not transpire, the Jehovah's Witnesses claimed that God had come, if in a more subtle way than foreseen, by releasing judgment on the earth—a view that conveniently incorporated the start of World War I into its apocalyptic scheme. In 1920 the organization published a small book with the bold title *Millions Living Today Will Not Die*, which claimed 1925 was the year in which Jesus would return, the faithful dead would be raised, and any obedient Christian alive would be transformed into a spiritual being. The book was widely distributed, and the ranks of the Jehovah's Witnesses swelled. But 1925 came and went without a visit from Jesus. After this, the Jehovah's Witnesses took a fifty-year break from making predictions. The year 1975 became the last failed prediction of the Jehovah's Witnesses to date.

Evangelicals consider the Jehovah's Witnesses a cult and are quick to denigrate and even mock these predictions and their subsequent reinterpretations. But even so, large swaths of evangelicals get caught up in date-setting schemes from time to time. When I was a teenager in the 1980s, I came across a booklet titled *88 Reasons Why the Rapture Will Be in 1988*, written by engineer and Bible student Edgar Whisenant. The book made the rounds to the tune of four million copies, and it was mailed for free to many pastors, including mine. The author was very good at finding links between numbers and dates in

GOD OF THE MIND   15

the Bible and in history and at drawing apocalyptic conclusions from them. My pastor was not impressed and tossed the booklet my way as a curiosity. When I first read it, I was a bit alarmed, but later it occurred to me that these were all just coincidences, and I thought that if a person was sufficiently motivated, they could probably find these sorts of coherences anywhere. It turns out I was right. When the prediction failed, Whisenant went through several cycles of updated prognostications that drew decreasing interest.

As Whisenant's light faded, popular evangelist and radio preacher Harold Camping began to take up the torch. It seems that once people start to predict the end of the world, each failure simply becomes a reason to try again. Camping first predicted Jesus would return on September 6, 1994. Then later on he named May 21, 2011 as the day of reckoning. This prediction made a very large splash with the American public, perhaps because people enjoyed sharing or mocking the story online, but also because of the large publicity campaign Camping's organization deployed. As if the end of the world needed a PR campaign! At first, Camping tried to reinterpret the failure as a spiritual event. But he later retracted everything and announced the end of his doomsday predictions. This prediction, at least, was accurate.

Most evangelicals take refuge in a very narrow distinction to separate themselves from unhinged end-of-the-world date-setters. They point out that Jesus said no one would know the date or the hour of his return (Matthew 24:36), and this seems to put their expectation of the return of Jesus in a different category. It's "soon," but we don't know *how* soon. However, they still maintain that Jesus could return at just about any moment and they also follow contemporary events to find clues that align with biblical prophecy. This is why every time there is a conflict in the Middle East, evangelicals write and consume books on this topic by the carton. These books explain how each participant on the world stage is alluded to in the Bible, what role they are destined to play, and how it will all come to a supernatural climax imminently. It doesn't seem to bother these Bible prophecy buffs that these striking alignments have been discerned for many generations, with nothing to show for them. Like fortune cookies, their predictions are so general that they could apply to almost any time in history.

The most popular version of end time events involves the "pretribulational rapture," meaning that all believers could disappear literally at any moment and be taken up into heaven, just in time to escape God's judgment upon the earth in the form of wars, pestilence, and other terrifying developments. The details are sketchy, but apparently nothing remains on earth of the raptured individuals but the piles of clothing, teeth fillings, and prosthetics left behind.

But is there a significant distinction between setting a date for the end of the world and believing it could happen at any moment? Both are equally wacky and highly questionable ideas. There is nothing but the writings of an ancient book to suggest that this is even remotely possible. Nothing in our current experience supports it, and in practice most evangelicals go about their daily lives on the assumption that the end is not actually imminent. They have mortgages, sign contracts, take on careers, make life choices, and plan for retirement. What experience *does* tell us is that people who have expected a supernatural end of the world have been wrong every single time. This doesn't mean the rapture can't happen (far be it from me to predict the future!), but how many other things have been predicted as imminent for two thousand years, never came to pass, and are still expected to happen?

WHY IS JESUS TAKING SO DARN LONG?

We can see the same pattern of predictive fails and reinterpretations in the Bible itself. Jesus seems to have believed that the kingdom of God was about to break through with supernatural power within the lifetime of his first followers.

- On one occasion, after mentioning his glorious future return with God the father and his angels, Jesus says, "I tell you the truth, some who are standing here will not taste death before they see the kingdom of God come with power" (Mark 9:1 cf. Matthew 16:28, Luke 9:27).[1]
- After describing the events leading up to the end of the world and his own return, Jesus says, "Truly I tell you, this generation will certainly not pass away until all these things have happened" (Mark 13:30 cf. Matthew 24:34, Luke 21:32).
- When Jesus gives his disciples instructions for preaching in his name, he finishes up with "I tell you the truth, you will not finish going through the cities of Israel before the Son of Man [Jesus] comes" (Matthew 10:23).

These are explicit statements and because of this they are puzzling to many modern Bible readers. But the Bible itself also provides explanations for these "apparently" failed predictions, and as in the case of more recent end-of-the-world date setting, the Bible also puts forward spiritual events and reinterpretations as alternatives when the literal expectation is foiled.

After Jesus died and was raised from the dead, the book of Acts says that he appeared to his disciples, and they asked him if it was now time to inaugurate the kingdom of God. This is a very interesting moment in the story, particularly if we read it from a non-miraculous, secular perspective. What is happening here, and why are the disciples asking this question? The reason is that early Jesus followers believed Jesus would return within his own generation with the kingdom of God in tow, to judge the world and usher in a new supernatural age. But by the time the books of the New Testament were being written, his followers were keenly and uncomfortably aware that Jesus had not returned as predicted. Enter the post-prediction fail adjustment. The answer that Jesus gives to his disciples is that "It is not for you to know the times or dates the Father has set by his own authority." Then Jesus tells them that for the foreseeable future, they will be preaching the gospel through the power of the Holy Spirit. Supernatural splendor is replaced with a decidedly this-world task. No angels, no billowing clouds of glory, no judgment of the world. Just, "go out and preach." It would have been fair for the disciples to push back a little and say, "Hey wait a minute, Jesus. You said this kingdom was happening imminently, but now suddenly you start talking about how only God knows the hour! This feels like bait and switch!" But of course, disciples don't get to talk back to Jesus, especially in manufactured dialogs.

So, to review:

Early in the first century Jesus says, "I'm coming back in glory imminently." Or at least, that's what his first followers believe.

Then he doesn't (*obviously*).

Then, later in the first century, the biblical author of Acts puts the question everyone is thinking into the mouths of the disciples in order to provide reassurance to his readers: "Why didn't Jesus come back?" The answer is, "Only God knows when Jesus is coming! Let's change the subject and talk about preaching the gospel."

Similarly, in the famous "great commission" passage in the Gospel of Matthew, Jesus tells his disciples that now, after his resurrection, he has all authority (Matthew 28:18). It sounds like it's time for that glorious kingdom to come down from the sky. I mean, what do you need that is greater than *all authority*? Let's get this show moving! But instead, Jesus tells his disciples that their job now is to teach the nations to obey his commands. And this would seem to imply a very long wait indeed, since teaching the whole world about him is no small task. Once again, a divine manifestation is deescalated to something less explicitly apocalyptic. Jesus now has all authority, but you'll have to take that on faith. And that imminent return? Well, there's a new agenda now.

The problem persists throughout the New Testament, and it even has a technical theological term in scholarly circles, *the delayed Parousia*. It refers not only to the problem of the delayed return of Jesus, but also the fact that the authors of the Bible are themselves aware of it and deploy various explanations to cope with it. The Apostle Paul seemed to think that Jesus could return at any moment in his early epistles, where, for example, in 1 Corinthians 7 he counsels people to avoid marriage and to hold their attachments to this world lightly, because "this world in its present form is passing away" (1 Corinthians 7:31). But in his later epistles the expectation is less imminent. In the book of Philippians, written towards the end of his life, he has adjusted, and he now meditates on what it means to live for Christ with a view to death, not the imminent intrusion of the kingdom of God. According to him, the kingdom of God had come in some sense with the death and resurrection of Jesus. But a fuller and —finally(!)—supernatural transformation of the entire creation was at hand and might happen at just about any moment.

In the epistle of 2 Peter, the author responds to "scoffers" who say, "Where is this 'coming' he promised?" The fact that the author addresses this issue must surely mean it was a sore point. He offers this explanation for the delay:

> But do not forget this one thing, dear friends: With the Lord a day is like a thousand years, and a thousand years are like a day. The Lord is not slow in keeping his promise, as some understand slowness (2 Peter 3:8-9).

But this is yet another spiritual reinterpretation of a failed prediction. God works on a different time scale, says the author, so much so that he is not very good at communicating about it. When he says "a minute" he might mean a couple weeks, and so forth. But the key point is that all this information is only made available to believers *after* the prediction failed to come about in a reasonable amount of time. This should sound familiar by now.

In all these examples we see the authors of the Bible themselves doing their best to cope, like the Jehovah's Witnesses and the Seventh Day Adventists, with the reality that Jesus and his earliest followers were expecting a swift conclusion to the story, and that this swift conclusion did not materialize. By the time the authors of the Bible were writing about Jesus in the middle to late first century, this was already a point of discomfort. So they introduced exculpatory ideas into the text, while at the same time attempting to be faithful to the Jesus tradition: It turns out Jesus didn't really mean a literal and quick return, even if it seemed that way; or it was about the power to preach the gospel, not about a literal return; or it was because God has a different time scale.

All these rationalizations don't get a lot of scrutiny as rationalizations from Bible-believing Christians because they are in the text of the Bible and as such they are treated as authorized explanations of the (somewhat confusing) divine timeline. But the pattern does resonate. It is hard to deny that they are not so different from the rationalizations that other end-time predictors have come up with to explain their predictive fails. First, predict an imminent and literal end of the world. Then, when it doesn't happen, provide some sort of spiritual sounding explanation or reinterpretation. The pattern is clear and embarrassingly effective. It is a mental trick that just keeps working year after year and century after century.

But the earliest Christians were not alone in their conviction that the end was near. The discovery of the Dead Sea Scrolls in 1947 revealed a group of Jews, roughly contemporary to Jesus, who had fled to the desert, were convinced that they were

God's chosen people living in "the last days," and were waiting for his vengeance to fall on the rest of the world. Their leader, referred to as the Teacher of Righteousness, interpreted the prophecies of the Hebrew Scriptures as though they applied to that moment in time to his little band of sectarian desert fanatics. They even calculated times based on biblical prophecies, landing on 177 BCE as the year in which God would return, through the work of their community. But this did not work out, leading to a couple updates that added 40 years in total. And after that, the predictions seem to have ceased. Like Jesus and later his followers, they expected a great conflict between themselves and the forces of evil—a tribulation, to be followed by the victorious return of God and the inauguration of a blessed age where righteousness reigns. In short, many of the teachings of Jesus regarding the end of the world and the coming of the kingdom of God were already found in outline form in the Dead Sea Scrolls, most of which were written before his birth. This suggests, again, that Jesus really did think the end was near, just like his contemporaries who said the same things. What if Jesus was a man of his times, whose imagination was prodded by the failed apocalyptic ideas of his contemporaries? What if Jesus, like the Harold Campings of more recent generations, also found in the failed predictions of others the impetus for his own?

A RELIGIOUS FANTASY

If I ask myself, "Why did I have that dream about the end of the world back then?" these are the facts that bubble up to the surface and so, I suppose, my doubts arose from my exposure to these ideas. Even though I consciously resisted the conclusions they seemed to point to, my subconscious was working away at them with a determined inevitability. It was initially very difficult to even think my unorthodox thoughts. And writing them down was even harder. It felt like I was doing something sinister and evil. At the same time, it felt intrepid too. Striking out into the unknown.

> How dare I even entertain these thoughts?
> *Well, I guess I'm doing it. Here goes….*
> Do I want to anger God? Won't I end up in hell?
> *But is he even there to be angry with me?*
> Won't my friends judge me? Won't my family be disappointed in me?
> *Why all the fuss? I'm just pursuing valid ideas that spring from facts.*
> Still, but what if he is there? "It is a terrible thing to fall into the hands of an angry God."
> *I said I wouldn't ignore my doubts anymore. And that's what I'm doing. Decision made!*

Some days I would achieve a sense of equanimity about my thinking. "There. I've done it. I'm out of the closet, at least to myself. This is me now. I'm okay with this. I have clarity." But then the next night lying in bed, I would be overcome with insecurity. Like a hiker who has ventured too far from civilization and is running out of food. "This is nuts. What am I *doing* out here? Why did I even think this was a good idea?" Panic, discouragement. But then again, "No! Steel your determination. This is the right path. There is no good reason to stray from it. These are only the ghosts of faith flitting about in your brain." These are the intense psychological pressures at work in the minds of sincere believers. Even the attempt to be open-minded and fair with the information is surrounded by noise and existential threats, like the question, "Does my spouse not love me?" It's too big. The implications are too massive; it just can't be faced. The conscious mind shies away from scandalous conclusions and tries to avoid them. But the subconscious has no such qualms.

Clearly, it is not the evidence itself that has created the

powerful conviction that Jesus is about to return at any moment. The credibility of his return is based on the stories that believers keep telling each other every single week at church, at prayer meetings, at youth group, at Bible study, in books, on YouTube channels and radio programs, and in personal conversation. This constant input forms the mind, perhaps even the brain itself. *This is your brain on religion*. The core beliefs of evangelicalism are not a result of information that comes from the real world of cause and effect. They are ideas that are compellingly passed on from person to person and generation to generation. These beliefs are first and foremost a construct of the mind.

There are many somewhat credible end-of-the-world scenarios in the non-religious realm. Most of them have been made into summer blockbusters, because apparently, we humans like to sit around and imagine what abject terror and utter destruction would look like.

- An asteroid could hit the earth and kill us all.
- The sun could spit out a massive flame of fire and scorch us.
- A plague could turn us all into zombies and we would die eating each other.
- Plants could stop growing properly, and we would starve and suffocate.
- There is always global warming.
- And of course, a variant of the common flu could wipe most of us out, ending the world as we know it.

All these scenarios—even the zombie apocalypse—are more credible than the idea that Jesus will return in glory. They are all extrapolations of the world as it now is. There are such things as asteroids and it's within the realm of possibility that a very large one could hit the earth. The threat of global warming is based on projecting current observations into the future. The zombie apocalypse is a bit of an outlier, but it is based on the reality of contagious diseases—depending on what kind of zombies we are talking about. Dead people coming back to life, no. But people overcome by a version of rabies? Not entirely impossible. Oh, and I forgot to mention aliens. Arguably, aliens could exist. And if they did, they would either be friendly or hostile, the latter resulting in yet another world-ending scenario. But the return of Jesus is not based on any information about the way the world works. There is just nothing to go on. Nothing shows it to be likely, nothing suggests a mechanism, there aren't even any precedents of similar things happening which might be appealed to. If we asked an evangelical why they believed in the return of Jesus, they would trace the authority like this: The return of Jesus is taught in the Bible, which is the word of God. Therefore, it must be true. But then, why is the Bible to be taken as the word of God? That one is a bit harder to answer. Expert apologists know about such things, but the average person in the pew isn't usually conversant with those issues. Ironically, one of the answers that apologists give for proving that the Bible is the word of God is that it contains many fulfilled prophecies! As we have seen, the authors of the Bible had no trouble changing the nature of the thing that is being predicted in order to squeeze a prophetic fulfillment out of it.

FUTURE PROOF

On the other hand, though, perhaps there is something about the observable world that explains the *conviction* that the end is near. The frustration of believing things which cannot be seen or proven needs an outlet, it needs something at least quasi-tangible to persist. The human mind can take a lot of subterfuge, but there are limits, and cognitive dissonance is bound to lead to a resolution. Because of this, believers are primed to accept the idea that the future will vindicate the unprovable beliefs of the present. "It's not seen to be true now, but just wait! You will see! The future will vindicate us!" The nice thing about the future is that it cannot be subjected to factual analysis. It is safe and secure from skeptical inquiry. No one can prove the future is wrong.

Well, I suppose that is precisely what I am trying to do by pointing out that if an idea of the future is the product of cognitive dissonance and comes with a long string of failed predictions trailing along behind it, it's not a likely or possible future. The precursors to the idea of the supernatural end of the world are psychological. Once we see them as psychological, they lose their connection to the world that exists outside the mind and they must be treated as fantasies and wishful thinking, for that is exactly what they are.

Evangelical Christians manage to convince themselves that their version of the end of the world is different from the predictions made by fringe groups, wacky individuals like Harold Camping, and cults. But the return of Jesus is a wacky, fringy, and cultish religious fantasy in all cases, and nothing in our current experience or knowledge supports the idea that this is a likely outcome.

CHAPTER 3
GOD'S PLAN FOR YOUR LIFE

TESTIMONY SUNDAY

Sometimes, when I was still a Christian, I would show up for Sunday morning service with my family in tow and groan inwardly upon realizing that it was "testimony Sunday." This is when the portion of the service usually reserved for the sermon is opened up to anyone in the congregation to talk about how God has been working in their lives. I shouldn't be dismissive. These are real people trying to make sense of their journey through life on planet earth, and each one of their trajectories is as valuable as mine. The reason for my inner groaning, though, was that people who are not used to public speaking can sometimes go on and on, be overly emotional, or even incoherent. For someone with speaking experience it can be a trying thirty minutes or more.

A good testimony begins with a challenge (the more desperate the better) and ends with a God moment. The God moment need not be a literal miracle. Usually it isn't. It can just be an insight, or a feeling of God's presence, or a renewed sense of purpose. And so, on testimony Sunday people line up to explain to the congregation, sometimes in tears, the terrible challenges they have recently confronted and how, in one way or another, God "was faithful" through it all or how "God provided" for their needs. The ability to interpret one's personal history as a demonstration of God's loving, if at times mysterious, management of their lives is clearly a high priority for all these folks, and it is a key component of what it means to be an evangelical Christian. Perhaps it is even the entire point of being a Christian for many people. When evangelical Christians get together to talk about God and life and spiritual things, the testimony is the underlying format of the discussion.

A famous pamphlet that almost every evangelical Christian seems to be aware of states that "God loves you and has a wonderful plan for your life." Even though this is sometimes criticized or even gently mocked for being a little too simplistic, the phrase resonates deeply throughout the entire framework of evangelical faith and experience. It is not necessarily taken to mean that a Christian will have a happy life. Rather, the point is that the Christian will have *a life that makes sense*. Given the human hunger for meaning and significance, making sense might even be preferable to merely being happy. Because of this, for the evangelical Christian, it seems as though God is behind every major decision, challenge, and life change.

And there is never any bad guidance from God. If, for example, God leads a person to move to another city to start a new ministry, but the imagined ministry never pans out, then this is interpreted to mean that God's ways are mysterious. Not that God made a mistake, or that the person made a bad decision, or didn't really hear the voice of God. The phrases that one uses to cope with this situation are, "this is a challenge of patience from him." Or, "his timing is different than ours." But one never hears, "I thought I heard God's voice, but I was actually following a questionable idea of my own, which I attributed to God." Even though this is doubtless something that happens all the time. Personally, I think that hearing your own voice and calling it God is the *entire* explanation of the phenomenon. Going through life is tough. It's comforting to think that our decisions are tied to a greater plan and under the oversight of a greater planner. If it's just us, well, that's really intimidating. What if we can't pull it off? What if we have bad luck? What if other people are against us? But as the Bible says,

- "If God is with us, who can be against us?" (Romans 8:31).
- "He who began a good work in you will carry it on to completion" (Philippians 1:6).
- "The one who is in you is greater than the one who is in the world" (1 John 4:4).

These passages are used by evangelicals so often as personal reassurances that they spring to my mind instantly when I think about the topic. Our personal life drama gains enormous significance when we think of ourselves as participating in the grand plan of God. But there is a dark side of this too, as when believers feel like they don't have any guidance from God. They don't know what the plan is. Now what? Many evangelical Christians, often young people choosing a path in life, are paralyzed by indecision because they can't figure out what they are supposed to do. They haven't been taught to step out and make a decision on their own.

Another thought that is often expressed by evangelical Christians on testimony Sunday is that God "allows us to go through hard times." But there is always a reason for it. And so, if a person goes through a time of depression, they might question God's love. But after things get better, they will realize that God let them go through a time of unhappiness for any number of good results that are now available on the other side: to learn to rely on him, to become more patient, or because there was something better waiting.

WAS IT REALLY GOD?

I'm not sure when the switch was flipped, but there was a moment when I started to hear testimonies differently. I began to listen to the little voice of reason in my head, whispering, "These are just rationalizations. They don't prove anything. They are all based on a premise which controls them, but which is not in itself demonstrable, namely, *God has a plan for your life.* This we believe. Therefore, every event in our life must fit a narrative that shows that gracious plan at work." The problem with the idea that God is managing our timeline is that once it is onboarded it becomes unassailable. Once we accept the notion that God is in charge, there is no way to falsify it, for he is either clear in his management or he is mysterious. And that covers every possibility. But he is never wrong, or neglectful, or absent. Any tension the commitment to God's plan raises can easily be explained by mystery, learning, patience, or the need for trust. God's activity in our lives, therefore, is a notion that, once accepted, explains everything, even in the face of experiences which test it considerably.

Another explanation for the experience of people who "go through hard times" and "learn to rely on God" might simply be that after the initial shock of a difficult turn in life, they adjust. After becoming accustomed to the new situation, they become more flexible and find advantages in the new normal. We all have a bias towards seeing our lives as meaningful trajectories. Everyone does. Not just Christians.

So, is all this talk about how God supervises and guides our lives nothing more than a way of working out the meaning of human existence within a religious paradigm? It might only say something about us as humans, but nothing at all about God: We humans seek meaning and need an assist, even if from imaginary sources, to get us through times of transition. When we finally adjust to a new situation, there is a moment of acceptance, as though we can finally take a deep breath and relax.

Times of uncertainty and transition are emotionally intense and vivid moments, and the feeling that great forces are at work, for good or ill, hovers over them. And so, it is an easy step to think that God is supervising all these things, even though psychology on its own provides a sufficient explanation.

But if there is no God supervising our journey and we are all alone in the universe, I have no desire to ruin a useful framework that many find fulfilling—even if I consider it to be a fantasy. Fantasy has its place. On the other hand, I do object to the Christian insistence that real meaning and fulfilment can *only* be found in the trappings of their particular framework. Are Christians guilty of ruining the meaning of life for everyone else? "Only Jesus saves. Only in God can you have a fulfilling life and become what you are supposed to be. You must join us and be like us if you want to be meaningful." It's this deeply sectarian and exclusivist aspect of Christianity that is the most troubling, particularly when there is little evidence that Christians are doing anything different than everyone else. We are all looking for meaning; we are all spinning out stories that make life worth living. Sometimes desperately, sometimes with laughably silly narrative devices.

THE QUEST FOR MEANING

Former believers often hesitate to "ruin everything" for believers, who, we think, are living happily within a warm and comforting illusion while we are stuck with the unenviable task of staring down the void. It can seem more humane to let them be. But human existence is a deep mystery no matter how you cut it. It seems to me that it is very difficult to assess whether a metaphysical system like Christianity, on average, makes people happier (or more miserable) than any other system. Evangelical Christians think they are born into a tragically flawed creation, where eternal damnation awaits most of humanity. And even Christians who, because they are saved, are supposedly safe from this terrifying prospect, still have to deal with the possibility of the threat. In spite of their assured salvation, questions do linger: Perhaps they are wrong about being safe from hell, perhaps they are not true Christians. What if they lose their salvation? What if they sin too much? What if they (God forbid) *become atheists*? The fires of hell await. How is that somehow less existentially threatening than the notion that there is no God and that all meaning resides in humans themselves, and that consciousness ceases at death? For a Christian who is terrified by the prospect of hell, secular materialism might be the good news that brings peace and hope. No matter how you spin it, being human is a strange and perplexing story, walking here, as we do, among giants who can easily tread on us, be they inscrutable gods or the uncaring laws of the universe. And the question of which story brings individuals the greatest fulfillment is up for grabs.

I sometimes wonder whether most people even care about big picture issues, like if there is ultimate meaning, a God, or life after death. Whether *I* do. It seems to me that for the most part, we humans derive meaning from our daily routines and ordinary satisfactions and pleasures, some of which etch deeply enough into our consciousness to become seemingly transcendent: the progress of life, and the people we find ourselves connected to; our individual trials, accomplishments, and rewards; feeling appreciated and appreciating others.

There is the endless rise and fall of the seasons. Just when we are tired of summer, along come the fresh winds of fall, and we feel it is the perfect time to slow down and gather up around a fire and enjoy each other's company. But later, when the cold is beyond bearing, we are released, now full of energy, into the new life of spring. Everything is fresh and green! And we keep doing this year after year as if we were made for it. And we have been, literally, made from and for this cycle. Made to love it and forever be amazed and seduced by it.

And then there's sex. Isn't it interesting that one of the most intense experiences humans can have is exposure to each other? We are each other's meaning. We don't need any supernatural third party here. But perhaps we are so fascinated and fearful of each other that we must invent quasi-human entities to shield us from the sheer terror and beauty of being known and accepted by another. When we exult in God's love, aren't we really exulting in, or perhaps longing for, the acceptance of our human peers? And isn't that really all we ever wanted and ever needed? And wouldn't we all be happier if we just faced that reality squarely?

We are like any other animal. Biology moves a dog to its fascination with smells and territorial maintenance, to attention from humans, to running with other dogs without any conscious purpose except the joy of bathing in the chemical soup of its biological urges. This is life! Feel it! Do it! And when you are done, say, "I have run the good race, and I loved every minute of it." In the same way all the things that interest human beings are connected to our physical existence: reproduction, health, breathing, tasting, eating, hygiene, physical exercise, mental stimulation. Every one of these activities is sourced in our physicality—even thinking itself, which is the activity of an organ—and they are all exquisitely adapted, such that engaging in them is supremely rewarding, producing physical states that we find compelling, like satisfaction, happiness, excitement, curiosity, and more. I'm fairly certain it is these little things that matter most to us.

But then someone comes along and builds a grand metaphysical cathedral and claims that without it none of this has any meaning. Meaning, in this context, is associated with permanence. Anything that does not last forever, or is not connected to something that lasts forever, is meaningless. That seems to be the controlling premise. It sounds convincing to some people, and the metaphysical vision gets bundled up with "lower case" social and personal meaning that makes up everyday life: weekly gatherings with family and fellow believers, major yearly celebrations like Christmas and Easter, long-term friendships, and meaningful life transitions like birth, coming of age, marriage, having children, and death. You don't really have to believe the "upper case" Meaning story to enjoy all these things. You could assent to it, not think much about it, and just go along with whatever it is that your tribe is supposed to do while at the same time deriving great "lower case" meaning from the more mundane dimension of life. The fact is, we humans all mostly care about the same things, regardless of what religious or ideological system we might use to organize our thinking. And what we will be doing in a billion years (eternal life), or whether or who came up with the idea of the universe is not, on average, massively compelling. Most of us find our meaning in the impermanent realm of daily living, "running with the dogs." As far as we can tell, we are all biology, all cells and amino acids, DNA, and, well, *life*. It's biology all the way down. But somehow this configuration of chemicals is also capable, if properly primed, of feeling metaphysical dissatisfaction with itself. It's a kind of existential peevishness, a turning up of the nose to the wonder of physical existence, as if it's just not good enough.

But isn't it in fact wonderous to just be here in this moment, making our little plans and living our little lives? Like the squirrel who runs around gathering and burying nuts (and probably forgetting where he buried most of them), or the cat who spends the afternoon laying in the warm sun and calls that a good day, or the sparrow busily constructing its nest in spring, with little understanding of why she is even doing it in that tiny brain of hers. These activities might not be of any great interest to other animals, but for squirrels, cats, and sparrows, they are life. They are utterly compelling and worthwhile—however ephemeral. And so, to some greater intelligence our activities might also seem transitory and of little consequence in the grand scheme of things, or interesting and adorable in a patronizing sort of way. But to us they are life itself, and they are worthwhile. Isn't that enough?

CHAPTER 4
GOD'S TRAIN WRECK FOR MY LIFE

FACING FACTS

My life looks like the exact opposite of a plan. More like sabotage. I went to bible school to pursue a vocation in Christian ministry. There I met my wife, who purported to have similar inclinations. Then I went to seminary. I worked as a worship leader, ran a center for homeless youth, and worked as a minister with college students. I started two different non-profit Christian organizations. I got a second, advanced degree, in theology. I taught pastors and leaders. I hobnobbed with famous theologians and held my own. And yet, I was always broke, always feeling like an outsider to churches, never really gaining the financial or relational support sufficient to be sustainable.

It is commonplace in Christian circles to hear stories like mine as a prelude to a big miracle moment. "I was broke, suicidal, and ready to throw in the towel, then out of nowhere…" Fill in the blank: A big check arrived, I met someone who finally made it all work, I got a bunch of emails from random people all telling me the same encouraging thing. This is standard fare in sermon after sermon, not to mention on testimony Sunday. But for me there were no miracle stories. No big checks in the mail. No "divine connections" that put me on the right path for sustainability. In short, no feel-good testimony with a narrative fiat at the worst moment. Only the sinking feeling that this was all going nowhere. Finally, I moved to a different career just to survive.

Did God provide? It did not feel like he did. If I was thoroughly committed to the idea that God always provides, then I could surely point to the fact that I was never hungry, that I never lost my home, and no one in my family died. But that seems artificial. People who have not faced years of poverty-level income might wax eloquently about things like, "God only promises to feed and clothe you" (a common saying among Christians, based on Matthew 6) without any understanding of the true toll this kind of life can take, not only on oneself, but on a whole family. And this did weigh on me. It was particularly moving to hear my children talking about being poor. They were not judgmental or upset about it. But they naively thought that poverty was just the way we were. To them, being poor was like being tall or being bad at sports. They did not realize that, at least in our case, poverty was a direct result of my choices and that those choices were a direct result of my misguided trust in God. Because I sincerely believed that if I did the work of ministry, God would take care of me. This is what I had been taught, and I had seen many examples of it throughout my life. But I now realize there was some survivor bias at work, a cognitive error in which we only factor in successes, because we can perceive them, but we don't factor in failures, because they are not around to be perceived.

After 25 years of pursuing what I thought was a call to ministry, I decided to abandon it. When I told my wife, she told me she never loved me, and left. Any attempt to get a redemptive story out of this seemed fraught with difficulties. I guess I'm a little too practically minded. I expect the evidence to add up. I kept using the phrase "at some point," as in *"at some point I have to recognize that God did not provide."* Or *"at some point I have to realize this life of faith is going nowhere."* And it's clear my expectation that there ought to be tangible evidence of God's supervision of my story is itself a significant departure from the evangelical approach. Because for a typical evangelical Christian, God's supervision is a bedrock belief. It is a premise to be reasoned *from*, and it is not itself subjected to critical analysis. I suppose if I wanted to go back and undo my unbelief, that would be an important moment. The time I first embraced the phrase "at some point." Because that was when I decided to not put unconditional trust in the narrative that God has a plan for my life.

When I first revealed my matrimonial crisis at church, a man there prayed for me and encouraged me, working from the same testimony script that he was used to hearing. He said that someday the relationship between my wife and I would be something amazing, something to write about. And I don't think he meant the kind of writing I'm doing now. In fact, nothing of the sort has happened. Similar to my hopeless dream about the second coming of Jesus, I immediately realized the break between us was profound and the gap unbridgeable. I allowed myself to wish and fantasize about a different end for a time, ignoring that pessimistic outlook. But clearly, our relationship was going down. Like a lead zeppelin. No amount of testimonializing was going to change that. But maybe I still pined after my ex-wife—not so much because of any personal attachment I had to her, but rather because I was enamored of the idea that if she came back to me, it would make a wonderful story out of my life. It's always darkest before the dawn, I would have said. What a story that would have made for Testimony Sunday! And I even wonder sometimes if I might have unwisely rekindled that doomed relationship, had it been an option, just because of my earnest desire to live out the testimony narrative.

But *at some point*, one has to face facts. Well, I guess strictly speaking, this is not true. One can go about life permanently without facing facts. Many people do. But I do feel the weight of facts and experience. Now I only believe that our lives evolve and that we learn to deal with the changes, and that is about all there is to it. We all know in theory that some people die prematurely and others fail to achieve their goals for a host of reasons and circumstances. I can't deny the possibility that I am one of those stillborn lives. One of those who never made it, in the company of those who died without meaning. It would be illogical to imagine that this sort of meaninglessness only happens to others. But there is another possibility. What if the only way to believe one's life story has a coherent, greater meaning is to rely on non-demonstrable claims and causal inferences that strain credibility? What if no one's life really makes any sense without the imposition of an improbable narrative? The problem for me, in my experience of Christianity, was that I found facile explanations disheartening and depressing. In the end, it was a great relief to give up on that futile exercise, take a deep breath, dust off my shoulders, and stop trying to make sense of it all. When giving up on meaning is a relief, you know the system of meaning you have been chasing is just not working.

I WOULDN'T PUT UP WITH THAT

When I was in seminary I took a class on the history of revivals, those moments in the past in which people converted to Christianity *en masse* and it seemed like there was a special revelation of God at work, a special enthusiasm for spiritual things. The teacher was an Anglican college professor. He was a very humble and personable guy and I really liked him. He told us some of his personal journey. His lifelong dream had been to become an Anglican priest (the equivalent of a pastor). But he had some sort of mental health disorder. Obviously, he could function perfectly well in a college context. But the policy of the Anglican Church at that time was that people with his condition could not be priests. And so, his lifelong call to ministry was thwarted. Instead, he became a college professor, although that was clearly not his first choice. It was also clear this was a major issue in his life, and that he was plagued by feelings of disappointment. This man questioned God, his wise management, his purposes, and the church in which he lived and worked. And yet he continued to serve in that context, he continued to uphold the system that excluded and frustrated him, and he continued to believe in the midst of circumstances that put considerable strain on the validity of his belief. Some people, perhaps most Christians, would interpret this as a virtue. They might even be inspired. They would doubtless commend him, because this sort of commitment is the essence of faith: to believe where there is no evidence. As the biblical character Job put it after he had lost everything, "Though he slay me, yet will I hope in him" (Job 13:15). But when I saw his situation clearly, my reaction was to say to myself, "I would never put up with that. Why continue to uphold a system that is clearly trying to exclude you and produces so much pain in your life?"

So why did I do the very same thing to myself for so long?

It might now be clear why hearing every week at church about how God provides and guides became a source of irritation to me. When confronted with the repeated and often incoherent attempts of Christians to interpret life as a grand plan managed by God, I ended up feeling like I just wanted to leave through the side door and move on with my life, such as it was. It's bad enough to be scraping the bottom of the barrel of emotional and financial survival without some guy preaching at you to keep trusting no matter what. The imperative to trust just becomes an added mental burden in the midst of everything else. It's a question of bandwidth. "Can you just shut up for a moment," I would think, "and let me not believe while I'm trying to survive?" It's like when you have an accident and everyone comes around and starts asking you questions: "What happened? Are you alright? Are you hurt?" But you can't even respond because your whole body is just flooded with *pain*.

Why does God provide for all those other people who have wonderful testimonies, yet not for me? Why is it that the owner of a boatyard is rescued at the last minute with contracts "out of nowhere" that save his business and the jobs of his workers, but I'm still broke, and nothing but pure human effort, in the face of crushing emotional wounds, seems to get me ahead? Right about the time I heard that testimony about the boatyard owner I was pawning my thousand-dollar guitar, the nicest one I had ever owned, to fund my daughter's eighteenth birthday party. I only got a fraction of its value, and no, I never went back to reclaim it. Don't they realize that when they tell miracle stories about last minute rescues, they are setting a precedent and building an expectation? But those of us without the miracle ending don't ever get invited up to share. Who wants to hear a story without a punchline?

I actually toyed with the idea of sharing my frustration with my pastor and asking him if I could give a subversive testimony, one in which there was no moment of revelation, no good ending. But then I realized that everyone would just say that God would eventually come through. Testimonies without a happy ending fall in the category of "patience," or "God has not yet answered," or "mystery." That's the beauty of the whole system. You can never prove it wrong because there might be an explanation just around the corner. And the greater the tension, the more glorious the explanation will be. On the other hand, we humans are a forgetful bunch. The fact that God didn't seem to provide on one occasion eventually falls away into the background. We remember successes better than failures. New, more plausible, divine interventions come to the fore, and we focus on those instead.

I do realize that these are not new paths I tread. Job, the

already mentioned biblical character, had similar thoughts. He had done nothing wrong, had he? His suffering did not make sense to him. God's plan for *his* life did not make sense. And yet he stood firm and did not curse God for all the tragedy that God had brought upon him. But then again, in the end, after all his suffering, God does come through. Job does get a good testimony out of it. And he gets everything back, with interest.

> After Job had prayed for his friends, the LORD made him prosperous again and gave him twice as much as he had before. All his brothers and sisters and everyone who had known him before came and ate with him in his house. They comforted and consoled him over all the trouble the LORD had brought upon him, and each one gave him a piece of silver and a gold ring. The LORD blessed the latter part of Job's life more than the first (Job 42:10-12).

How convenient for Job and for the narrative. According to the book of Job, having God dump on you is a pretty good investment strategy. Double your income in a year! But can we really be so naive as to not recognize that many people come to the end of their lives without any coherent narrative to their name? Without any big moment of revelation? We are happy to lay the burden of proof on the future. And then, once a person dies, the question becomes less urgent. We don't know. Mystery. We don't care as much, to be perfectly honest, because it isn't us and it isn't a living person sitting in front of us asking for an explanation. The story, such as it was, is over. Death overtakes any questions about life. In this manner, the idea that God faithfully leads and provides for us is placed beyond all possible scrutiny.

BRING YOUR DOUBTS TO JESUS

I know some readers will be extremely irritated with me at this point. I thank them for sticking with me. They will dislike my insistence on outcomes or proof. They will say, that is the whole point of faith. You don't know, but you trust anyway.

But this *is* my key point. I am questioning belief itself. Why does anyone expect me to believe in something that can't be verified? Or something that doesn't at least have some sort of testability? And why is it considered morally reprehensible for me to disbelieve something which is not clearly based on experience, or which does not at least match my own experience? Isn't that weird? Would God expect this of me? Why? *Can someone please explain to me why I should not expect to see palpable evidence that God is working in my life?* The fact that my insistence on verification is treated as objectionable, sinful even, is itself concerning. I have to keep telling myself that it's not my fault that the evidence is lacking. It's not my fault that I disbelieve. It's not my fault that it doesn't make sense. The lack of sense is external to me. I did not create it in some spiteful metaphysical outburst. I am merely perceiving it. I have to tell myself this because I have internalized the message that doubt is bad. But who insists that doubt is bad instead of offering reasons? Probably those who do not have sufficient reasons to offer.

There is a fake generosity regarding doubt in evangelical circles. Pastors love to tell congregants that it's okay to have doubts; that doubt is part of belief. "You can bring your doubts to Jesus," it is said, "he will still accept you. You don't have to pretend. You can ask your tough questions."

And it sounds good. But can we *answer* our tough questions? Or do they just have to sit in a silo forever? We know this is fake generosity because the whole strategy is founded on the assumption that doubts are illusions which will dissipate. Even the idea of "bringing your doubts to Jesus" contains the contradiction. What if I doubt that Jesus even exists? How can I bring anything to him? What would that even mean?

> "Jesus, I'm pretty sure that you don't exist. Can you help me sort this out?"
> "You're right, I don't exist. Never had. Never will. Be at peace."
> Said Jesus never.

Obviously, the encouragement to "bring doubts to Jesus" (or God) contains the implication that the doubts are illusions. And if you do bring them to Jesus, as opposed to, say, Richard Dawkins, you are pretty much guaranteed to arrive at a certain kind of answer. And the magnanimous evangelical pastor who said it's OK to doubt has no idea what to do with the parishioner who evolves into a full atheist. Because Jesus doesn't accept atheists. That's just not an option. Now what? Well, I guess you just have to have faith, which is to say, you just have to continue to believe something you don't actually believe.

Some people's religious experience is coherent enough that it is easier for them to accept the notion of God's calling and supervision of their life. Things went well for them. Life followed an expected narrative arc. They got married and had kids. They got the job they always wanted. They became successful and grew old with their loving spouse. Were these people really exercising faith when they so clearly saw God's hand of blessing upon the story of their life? Their lives *do* make sense. That's not a statement of faith; it's a response to evidence. So apparently it's okay to respond to the *presence* of evidence and conclude from this that there is a God who is acting in your life, but it's not okay to respond to the *lack* of evidence and conclude that God is not doing anything at all. A clear case of a double standard if there ever was one. If life makes sense, "Praise the Lord! He has a wonderful plan at work!" If it doesn't make sense, "Be patient. The evidence will surface eventually."

Perhaps these blessed people have not ever encountered a life-shattering scenario which puts true tension on their ideas. On the other hand, I have to admit I have met people who have gone through some horrific things, things that make my complaints seem paltry, and this has only strengthened their faith. I don't know the answer to this. They never said the three words, *at some point*.

CHAPTER 5
THE GOD WHO DOESN'T SHOW UP

Back when I was trying to sort out what I really thought of people's testimonies, and whether they really show God at work or not, a crazy and very heretical thought popped into my head. A thought I could not unthink. What if the Bible itself is built on the same themes of the "testimony Sunday"? This sacred text sets up a vision of God's plan for the world so grand and compelling that vast swaths of humanity have accepted it, lock, stock, and barrel. And the authors of Scripture are themselves, of course, under the sway of this entrancing vision. But like any contemporary individual who sees their life through the prism of the testimony, the authors of the Bible are also faced with the inglorious reality of life on the ground, where the vast and glorious narrative doesn't seem to be working as planned. This is because the narrative is an illusion that has been created in order to provide a majestic backdrop to the drama of life. But instead of accepting that it is an illusion, the authors of the Bible manufacture explanations which are only credible to those who already share their commitment to the foundational premise: God loves us and has a plan for the world. The authors of the Bible accept this as axiomatic, and therefore, anything that happens proves it. If circumstances conspire such that it seems that God's plan is at work, as when under King David and King Solomon, Israel was for several decades the ascendant power of the region, that's proof of God's good plan. If God doesn't seem to be at work, as when Israel is repeatedly invaded and plundered by the empire of the day, then there is always some explanation, for this also proves God is at work.

And tying the themes together is faith. You don't need faith when God is standing right there in front of you. Faith only arises when the promise does not materialize. Faith is itself, then, evidence that the promise has failed. Or faith is the evidence that the promise is still coming. Potato—*potato*. The fundamental distinctive of the Judeo-Christian tradition is this: It makes intoxicatingly majestic proclamations about God, his thoughts and plans, but it can't deliver on them. And in the place of that failure to deliver, it introduces an apologia, or defense, that calls for faith.

THE EXODUS NARRATIVE

Starting with Abraham, God promises a great nation will come from him and that through it, God will bless the whole world. God also promises Abraham that his descendants will eventually possess the land in which he lives as a nomad. The same promise is reiterated to Abraham's progeny, but then the entire family, now a people in its own right, are enslaved in Egypt for four hundred years. The Bible makes much of the fact that God finally delivered on his promise some twenty generations later when he rescued them out of Egypt, as the story is told in the book of Exodus. But it always struck me as strange and inconvenient to the narrative that vastly more generations of Jewish slaves didn't see the promise fulfilled than did. For these people, it seems, God did not provide.

But the great liberation does finally come, and this is where the supernatural sparks start to fly. This is where God shows up. First, he sends the plagues, which basically destroy Egypt. Then the Israelites finally head out and God, through Moses, famously parts the sea with the Egyptian army at their heels. The pursuing army is then drowned when the sea is closed up on them. And the miracles just keep on coming. In their travels through the desert, if they run out of water, Moses makes water appear; if they run out of food, here comes a huge flock of quail to feed the nation. These are also the days of manna, a food that miraculously appears every morning, like the dew. In the day, God guides them with a cloud, and at night with a fire. Can you imagine? These people could look out at the horizon and say: "That's God out there, leading us." The climax comes when the tribes of Israel arrive at Mount Sinai and God moves in. There are flashes of lightning, dark clouds, and the sound of trumpets coming from the mountain. Pulling out all the stops here. The presence of God is thick and ominous. Then Moses goes up to the mountain and gets the Ten Commandments, straight from the hand of God, with the laws written by his very finger, and God shows Moses some of his glory. But Moses would die if he saw God's face, so he only gets to see God's back as God passes by. Later, Moses sets up a tent where he goes to commune with God, and every time he comes out, his face is glowing with reflected Glory.

This is all heady stuff. The glory of God. The numinous. The Other breaking through. We're talking about over a million people wandering around in the desert in a miracle-saturated environment. It is an amazing narrative. And when I used to believe it, I found it fascinating and motivating. But of course, I now no longer think this is a historical account. This is literature. While I don't doubt its ancient readers thought it was true, just as many modern Christians do, it seems to me the appropriate response to an ancient text that describes miracles on this scale is a heavy dose of skepticism. After all, we have zero confirming evidence, and we aren't even sure exactly when the biblical books that describe these events were written, let alone when the events were supposed to have happened. But the reason I've spent the time to paint this picture is that this exodus narrative is the baseline for the rest of the Hebrew Scriptures. Everything that follows looks back to it, not just as a series of past events, but as a hope and a promise: If God did this in the past, he can do it in our time.

But I've left something out of the description of the Exodus, which also becomes a guiding theme through the rest of the books of the Old Testament. This magnanimous revelation of divine power and care is continually marred, almost from the very start, by the idolatry, hard heartedness, and the lack of faith of its would-be recipients. When Moses goes up to Mount Sinai to receive the Ten Commandments, he is gone for forty days. Apparently this made everyone nervous, and their response was to make a golden calf, which they worshiped and celebrated. This is happening at the very same moment that God is etching the sacred laws into stone. So, understandably, both God and Moses are angered by this blatant idolatry, and God wants to kill everyone (the story implies that we are talking about some 1.5 million people) and start all over with just Moses. Moses talks God down from the edge—but there's still a massacre of the most prominent offenders. The message is clear: You have to be faithful to God —Yahweh, the one that rescued you from Egypt—if you want to enjoy his blessings. And if you aren't faithful, it will be your own fault that God doesn't do all the wonderful things he said he would do. This is a recurring theme throughout the Exodus:

- The people complain about their trials in the desert and God sends a fire that burns some of them, but Moses again intercedes and the fire subsides (Numbers 11:1-3).
- The people tire of manna and they want some meat. So God sends them a massive flock of quail, but at

the same time, he peevishly makes them sick when they eat it (Numbers 11:4-34).
- Moses sends twelve spies to explore the region the Israelites plan to invade— "The Promised Land." Of course, people already live there, and ten of the spies are intimidated by what they see and report that there's no way the Israelites will be able to conquer them. The nation as a whole backs away from the project based on this report. Because of their lack of faith, God curses them all to live in the desert for forty years, until the generation of doubters dies out. He again threatens to kill everyone and start over with Moses, but he is once again talked out of it (Numbers 13-14).
- Moses himself gets in hot water when he does not follow God's instructions to the letter in getting water to flow from a rock. As a result, Moses will not be allowed to enter the promised land (Numbers 20:6-12).
- The people once again complain about the food and the lack of water, leading God to send a plague of snakes, killing many. Then Moses casts a bronze snake with the power to heal anyone who looks at it (Numbers 21:4-9).

The message from all these horrific stories is clear enough: God is ready to reveal himself, but the rebellion, grumbling, and lack of faith of his people stand in the way of this magnanimous offer. If this was not clear enough from these accounts in the exodus narrative, it becomes crystal clear in the book of Deuteronomy, which is dedicated to the theme of obedience: If you worship God and follow his commands, he will bless you. If you don't, he will curse you. Deuteronomy actually previews the entire history of the nation of Israel that is later recounted in the rest of the Hebrew Bible, interpreting it in the paradigm of obedience/blessing and disobedience/curses, suggesting it was not written before the historical books, as is purported, but after. The formula—good outcomes if you obey, bad outcomes if you disobey—is repeated again and again (see Deuteronomy 28 for a good example). And so the question arises: Isn't the idea that disobedience keeps God's blessings at bay an apologia for why, in spite of the great love and awesome power the scriptures proclaim, God doesn't actually show up? Doesn't this idea function as an explanation for why all the miracles of the exodus narrative manage to stay on the pages of Scripture and never break through into real life? Israel was supposed to bless the nations, and on the metaphor of a priestly calling, it was supposed to be the purveyor of God's love and grace to all humans. But it is painfully obvious to the biblical authors that Israel is not blessing anyone and that no one is recognizing their priestly calling. Why? And isn't this the exact same frustration and conundrum that both Jews and Christians have been dealing with for millennia, be it on a personal or cosmic scale? Their God makes grandiose claims, but then he doesn't show up. And when this happens, people have two options. Either give the whole thing up and admit that *at some point* it all becomes incredible (which is to say unbelievable, as in something you cannot put faith in), or come up with an explanation that props up the premise, even if it is tendentious, facile, and self-flagellating.

To be perfectly clear, my claim here is that the accusation of rebellion is a subsequent explanation that is manufactured after the promise has failed to materialize. Like the reinterpretations of the end of the world that we saw in chapter 2, this accusation rescues the idea of God's promise by placing the blame on its would-be recipients.

THE PROPHETS

A passage in Isaiah is worth quoting at length because it shows so clearly how eager biblical authors are to take on and assign blame when things go wrong. Notice the longing for a revelation like the one described in Exodus in which God breaks through to this world and is visibly present with his people. But then notice how quickly the blame turns to the people of the nation, who have been, it is claimed, unfaithful to God. It is their fault that God has not revealed himself.

> Oh, that you would rend the heavens and come down,
>   that the mountains would tremble before you!
> As when fire sets twigs ablaze
>   and causes water to boil,
> come down to make your name known to your enemies
>   and cause the nations to quake before you!
> For when you did awesome things that we did not expect,
>   you came down, and the mountains trembled before you.
> Since ancient times no one has heard,
>   no ear has perceived,
>   no eye has seen any God besides you,
>   who acts on behalf of those who wait for him.
> You come to the help of those who gladly do right,
>   who remember your ways.
> But when we continued to sin against them,
>   you were angry.
> How then can we be saved?
> All of us have become like one who is unclean,
>   and all our righteous acts are like filthy rags;
> we all shrivel up like a leaf,
>   and like the wind our sins sweep us away.
> No one calls on your name
>   or strives to lay hold of you;
> for you have hidden your face from us

and have given us over to our sins (Isaiah 64:1-7).

This tug-of-war between obedience/blessing and disobedience/cursing is the entire theme of the prophetic books of the Old Testament, which take up about one third of that section of the Bible: Bad things have happened or are about to happen because we have abandoned God. But if we return to God, he will flood us with his presence and his blessings. Open any prophetic book at random and you are likely to land on this sort of assessment. The book of Jeremiah, which is a recounting of the message of its eponymous prophet, is an unrelenting screed against the people of Jerusalem who, because they worshiped Baal instead of the Hebrew God, and because they disobeyed their God's rules for life, were about to be invaded by the armies of Babylon.

> Look! He advances like the clouds,
>> his chariots come like a whirlwind,
>> his horses are swifter than eagles.
> Woe to us! We are ruined!
> O Jerusalem, wash the evil from your heart and be saved.
> How long will you harbor wicked thoughts?
> A voice is announcing from Dan,
>> proclaiming disaster from the hills of Ephraim.
> "Tell this to the nations,
>> proclaim it to Jerusalem:
> 'A besieging army is coming from a distant land,
>> raising a war cry against the cities of Judah.
> They surround her like men guarding a field,
>> because she has rebelled against me,'"
> declares the Lord.
> *"Your own conduct and actions*
> *have brought this upon you"* (Jeremiah 4:13-18).[1]

And this is no mere rhetoric either. As expounded in this,

well, *jeremiad*, the armies of Babylon are on their way. Eventually, they do come and invade, and they take a significant portion of the people of Israel into exile. The book of Jeremiah is followed by the smaller book of Lamentations, which mourns the loss of a whole nation after Jerusalem and its surrounding area has been devastated by the Babylonians because the people did not remain faithful to God. You can see in the message of the prophets the way in which God's goodness, care, and plan for the nation of Israel are placed beyond all possible falsification. First, as we have seen, is the blame game: God wanted to bless us, but we were too bad. So, in spite of all these terrible things that are happening, God is still good! It's all our own fault, our own fault, our own fault. Unquestioning belief in the good plans of an imaginary deity will always, inevitably, and with complete predictability lead to the conclusion that when things go wrong, it is our own fault. And things will always go wrong in one way or another.

A second response is the reinterpretation game. Things are not as they seem. It might seem like the nation is being threatened by an unstoppable military force, one so great that not even God can control it. Remember how God drowned the Egyptian army? Why isn't he doing it now? Is he not powerful enough? Has he forgotten his promise? Why doesn't he just snap his fingers and kill every single soldier in an instant? He does have the power to do so, right? But God's purposes and power are an unassailable bedrock. That must remain true, even if it makes everything else false. And so enters the rationalization: *God is using this mighty military machine for his own purposes!* They can only invade us because they have God's permission and blessing to do so. (The fact that they are, objectively speaking, an awesome and unstoppable military force has nothing to do with it at all!) You can see that at work in the passage from Jeremiah quoted above. It starts by describing how God is advancing against Jerusalem with a supernatural army, and it ends with a description of a besieging army from a distant land. These armies are not coming against God, says Jeremiah, they are working for him! Similarly, in a previous cycle of invasions, when the Assyrians defeated northern Israel, they are referred to as the rod of God's anger, and the club of his wrath (Isaiah 10:5). But they are bad too and will eventually get their own.

IF MY PEOPLE

An interesting question in all of this is whether the accusations of the prophets against the victims, the people of Israel, are historically accurate. The two-fold indictment is that the people of God have been worshiping other deities, Baal in particular, and that they have also committed a host of injustices such that society is a complete and utter moral cesspool. To what extent, one wonders, is this assessment driven by the apologia rather than by the daily reality of life on the ground in ancient Israel? Even today, there are evangelical Christians loudly decrying the evils of our own society. Things are always getting worse, judgment is always around the corner, Jesus is coming soon because God can't let this go on much longer. But are things really that bad? On further investigation, the sorts of behaviors that lead to this apocalyptic assessment are things like gay marriage, sexual freedom, divorce, and the prohibition of prayer in schools. These assessments are heavily influenced by a particular religious and ideological take, and not everyone else agrees that the world is going to hell over these particular issues. It doesn't seem like a stretch to imagine that all the moral depravity perceived by the prophets of the Hebrew Scriptures was just part and parcel of their unwavering commitment to the exodus narrative. "If things are going sideways, it must be that we are being bad," can easily become a source of confirmation bias. What if the people of Jerusalem were not more or less bad than anyone else living in the Levant circa the first millennium BC—just trying to get through life, and then, when they are faced with the existential threat of invasion, they also have to deal with this jerk of a prophet who won't shut up about how bad they are.

When Christians complain about the moral slippery slope of society, as they have been doing for centuries, aren't they mostly following the lead of Jeremiah and the other prophets and then cherry-picking a few contentious examples? The path to a prophetic moral assessment goes like this:

1. God is pure love and all good intentions, super powerful, and beyond any and all criticism.
2. Therefore, when God is unaccountably inactive or seemingly uncaring, it is not his fault.
3. There are only two parties here. God and us. It's not like we're going to blame whales or aliens. Therefore, when God is inactive, it is our fault.
4. Since we must have done something to deserve God's lack of action on our behalf, we must be bad, and we must be doing bad things. Look! There is a bad thing people are doing!

This sort of reasoning helps explain something that outsiders to evangelical Christianity don't always understand. They wonder why Christians are so bent on imposing their moral behaviors on others. The rest of the world tends to say, "If you don't like abortions, then don't get one. If you don't agree with gay marriage, don't marry someone of the same sex. Why are you so intent on forcing this on others? What is the problem and what gives you the right to do so?" The problem is that evangelical Christians believe that God is assessing the future of the nation based on its total moral capital, just as was the case in ancient Israel. And in that scenario, everyone's moral behavior matters, not just the behavior of Christians. And so, the insistence that everyone bow to Christian morals is ultimately sourced in a selfish concern which boils down to this: "You being bad will make things bad for me when God judges our nation for its depravity."

Evangelicals love to cite a passage from 2 Chronicles, one of the historical books of the Old Testament:

> If my people, who are called by my name, will humble themselves and pray and seek my face and turn from their wicked ways, then will I hear from heaven and will forgive their sin and will heal their land (2 Chronicles 7:14).

There are songs based on it, commemorative plates, and wall hangings. And it is endlessly quoted in books and sermons. In context, it is the word of God to King Solomon after the completion of the temple that he built, and it faithfully follows the obedience/blessings and disobedience/curses pattern. The line from the apologia of the authors of the Hebrew Scriptures right through to contemporary culture wars and politics is unmistakable and quite easy to follow, as the introduction a YouTube user appended to a popular song rendition sums up nicely:

> In light of all the tragic events that have recently occurred, namely the earthquakes in Haiti, Chile, and China to name a few, I would like to dedicate this video to all the survivors. I would also like to send this video out to America. We have gotten so far removed from what this nation was founded upon The WORD of GOD! My hope is that America turns back to GOD whole heartedly! Contrary to popular belief, God is SPEAKING (HE's speaking by way of a FAILED ECONOMIC SYSTEM, a down trotten AUTO Industry and the worst JOB Market since World War II) He's saying REPENT and HE will heal this land.[2]

In other words, we must be faithful to the Judeo-Christian moral vision as expounded in the Bible, if we want our country to continue to enjoy God's blessing. Presumably, Chile, China, and other nationalities must also do the same. Can it really be that the largest economy in the modern world is being held hostage by an imaginary God, invented by a handful of ancient prophets and scribes? Can it really be that our moral discourse today, right here in the 21st century, is being stymied by the demands of a petty Middle Eastern deity who quite simply does not exist? If Moses, assuming he was a real person, could see the awesome power his ideas were yielding now, thousands of years later, in a world that would be otherwise incomprehensible to him, he would surely be incredulous, and maybe a little bit proud. But we also should be incredulous, which is to say unbelieving, of this ancient vision, for its failed predictions, backward ideas, and the way it denigrates our humanity by telling us that we are bad and that we are the cause of the tragedies that strike us. These ideas only survive on the back of the desperate human hunger for transcendent meaning.

The idea that when bad things happen it's our own fault was finally and decisively put to the test in the 20th century during the Holocaust. Without denigrating the experience of other persecuted peoples, the Holocaust was a special case given its brutally efficient bureaucratic approach to murder and the sheer number of humans who were destroyed by the Nazi machine (some six million Jews died), but also as a striking theological drama. Here are the people who were formed by the blessings/curses narrative, which through Christianity has become such an influential factor in human consciousness. The Holocaust was the ultimate showdown between God and humans: the greatest claim of God's goodness up against the most depraved acts of evil. The question here is tragically and horrifically pointed. According to the biblical narrative, God will bless and protect the Jews so long as they are faithful to him. To uphold that narrative, we would have to say that the six million Jews who died in the Holocaust did so because they were unfaithful to God. But can we really say that? Under the strain of this situation, the pattern of blessings/cursings strains and, for many, it breaks, and is revealed to be the illusion it always was. There are limits. We humans can only bow to our sadistic imaginary gods for so long. Our capacity for bearing cosmic guilt is not limitless. No amount of idolatry, if there were such a thing, would merit a Holocaust. And Jews as a people were and are no more guilty of sin, if there is such a thing, than the average human being. No one deserves that. The Holocaust should be the final nail in the coffin of the exodus narrative and its pattern of obedience/blessings and disobedience/curses.

CHAPTER 6
THE GOD WHO DOESN'T HELP

STREET THEOLOGY

One of my projects as a Christian minister was to run a drop-in center for street kids. I was ill-suited for the job: an intellectual whose favorite pastime was to sit around and talk about theology and philosophy. What did I know about helping kids who had mental illness, addiction, broken families (sometimes all three together), and on top of that were homeless? A funny fact about Christian ministry is that people seem to think expertise in the Bible translates into expertise about a whole bunch of other things. But just because I can tell you what Jesus said about helping the poor does not mean I'm good at it myself! The previous director of the same center had been my polar opposite: rotund, warm, engaging, generous with hugs, and with a sunny disposition. Everyone loved him. But I took the job out of a sense of duty. What good is all my theology, I thought, if it can't inform this most basic Christian task of taking care of the needy? So I focused on the things I did well, like getting volunteers trained and organized, and setting up respectful and safe standards. Things my predecessor had not excelled at. The other thing I was good at was, as

I mentioned, discussion. I could sit and talk about anything with anyone, asking questions, inserting my own opinions or ideas, and enthusing or empathizing as called upon. But I was a bit stingy with the hugs. Still am.

The ministry was not focused on evangelism. We just provided for physical needs and, through the volunteers, safe and friendly relationships. We did, however, leave the door open for questions about spirituality and God to develop. As seems to be the case universally with homeless people, so it was here: Most of our clients had prior experiences and ideas about God, the Bible, and the spiritual world. I've never been the sort of person to impose my ideas on others. In my perfect world, we have a good discussion, and all parties leave at least a little bit more enlightened.

One night I had a very memorable and puzzling experience. I and several other workers were talking to a teenager in our care about God. The topic had come up naturally and as he had expressed that he did not believe in God, we were all discussing the topic in a very friendly and open manner. But after a few minutes of this, and with all apparent sincerity, he went to the core of his problem with God. When he was younger, he said, his father would abuse and beat him. As a child he would run away, asking for God to help him. He had vivid memories of crying out to God in the moment of abuse to save him from his father. And I mean urgently, as in, he's running away from his dad saying, "God please help me!" But God never did save him. This should be familiar territory by now: The thwarted expectation that God, from what we know about him, ought to show up, but then he doesn't. And this primal experience had led him to the conclusion that God wasn't there. It wasn't a considered philosophical or rational assessment, but a very practical one: All I know is that God didn't show up for me when I needed him the most. That simple.

When he was done telling his story, I was at a loss for words. All I could do was tell him that it pained me a great deal and that I didn't have an answer that could explain it. He basically won the argument. I mean, when someone pulls out the "God didn't save me from my abusive father" card, the intellectual game is over.

SO MANY EXPLANATIONS

Now, many years later, I still find it a very compelling question: Why does God not interfere in a situation like that? I can't think of a *good* answer. I am of course theologically astute and educated enough to know the sorts of answers that defenders of the faith usually offer up. But are they good answers?

That God did rescue him, in a sense, because look, he's not getting beaten by his dad anymore. He's here among Christians, God's representatives, and he's safe. But that feels like a weak answer. It does provide the comforting notion that there are people in the world who care. But that's not the question. The question is, does *God* care? If the only evidence we can muster for God caring is that people who claim to be motivated by God care, then that is not hugely compelling. After all, it would not take much work to find a group of people who care, but don't believe in God. So maybe some people just care about others and that's the way some people are. People who believe in God attribute this characteristic to him, but who is to say where it comes from? And anyway, it's not like we had transformed this kid's life. He was still living on the streets. The key point is that God never answered in the moment of distress. Was God teaching this vulnerable child patience? Did this abused child need to learn trust? Or is the "God cares about us" framework just not strong enough to bear the weight of this pointed scenario? I'm sure we can agree that there are many other similar scenarios that place enormous pressure on the notion that God cares or provides. Like, for example, the shocking case of priests and youth pastors who commit child abuse, and who must be called to account by secular governmental authority.

Or the mass murders that take place every decade or so somewhere in the world, often religiously motivated.

Another popular response to the problem of God's passivity in the face of evil is to blame it on people. But the working premise is that God can do anything he wants to do, and that he hates to see people suffer. People do horrible things all the time. And they are to blame for those things. But this in no way mitigates the criticism leveled at God. He's the one in charge. He's the one with all the power. He's the one who set this all up. He can stop bad people from doing bad things if he chooses to do it. And the most basic problem here is the Christian claim that God himself hates evil. That is a potent idea, and it is one that requires some sort of demonstration in a world overrun by pain and abuse on any given day. But we don't get any demonstrations. We just get explanations.

But the idea that evil is the fault of humans is both Christian and biblical. In traditional Christian thought, the first humans rebelled against God and as a result they were expelled from the idyllic garden that God had made for them. They were then cursed to live outside of God's presence, impure, and now unworthy of his glory. According to the Bible all the horrible things that happen in the world, all the way from "acts of God" like earthquakes and volcanoes to human cruelty go back to the original sin of Adam and Eve. Here's the scenario: An all-powerful deity creates the world and puts people in it. The people immediately disobey a single command from this deity, involving what tree they can eat from. As a result, the millions of people who descend from these two individuals, over thousands of years, are cursed to endure all manner of suffering, including the murderous rampages of other people. Some of them, if they believe the deity, will be allowed to return to something like the original garden. But those who can't swallow this tale are condemned to eternal torment. I don't know whether to laugh at the absurdity of the tale or cry because so many people believe it.

Another explanation is that God meant the evil deed for a greater purpose, one which will become manifest at a later point. Well, that is not so much an answer as a possibility—a possible answer. One which throws the real answer off into the unknown future and is really an appeal to exercise faith and nothing more than that. Wishful thinking. The future will have the answer! A believer will be predisposed to view this more positively than a nonbeliever. Admittedly, some bad things do become the springboard for good things, as when someone who grows up in an abusive home is inspired by that experience to help others in the same situation.

But is it realistic to claim that all suffering is thus explained? Hardly. Many people suffer terribly and then die. Whatever good might possibly come out of that scenario won't benefit them. If it benefits others, then we have another issue: Does God sacrifice some people for the good of others? And wouldn't that itself be problematic?

And will eternity account for it? Hard to say. Once people die, the Christian worldview adds the complication of eternal destiny, and the cruel implication that if someone is going to hell, then all accounting for their suffering is a moot point. So what if you died during a gang rape? If you were going to hell anyway, this is just the beginning. You got to hell early, so to speak. Is that how we are to view God? He is a legalist who does not answer pleas from helpless children because they are going to go to hell anyway?

The most extreme view is to point out, as some Christians do, that everyone deserves hellfire anyway, so what's the problem? Just be grateful that God is saving some. While that has a logical tidiness to it, it rings hollow. It begs the question: "Why couldn't God have come up with a better system when he made the world? One that did not land the vast majority of humans in hell." It would appear that God was not capable of creating the world without creating evil. So he's not all-powerful after all? Or, on seeing that he could not create the world without human misery, why didn't he just skip the entire project? Or, when he did get around to saving some of the humans, why did he stop short and not save everyone? *Mystery.* Some ideas seem sensible when you are listening to educated-sounding theologians, but on further inspection they are shown to be downright bizarre.

A variation on the previous answer is to say that God did deal with evil once and for all when Jesus died on the cross for the sins of the world. His death and the forgiveness that comes from it, it is said, is the ultimate triumph over evil because now God can forgive all the evil people who believe in him. Someday (again, a future-oriented answer) all will be made right when God creates a new heaven and a new earth and "he will wipe every tear from their eyes" (Revelation 21:4). In this scenario, the street kid I was talking with a) doesn't get any help from God in this life and b) ends up in hell because he doesn't believe in God. But let's imagine that his dad went to an evangelistic crusade and believed in Jesus. Now his dad, who beat his child, ends up in heaven. And the beaten child who does not believe in God precisely because of his dad's actions ends up in hell. It's all just a bit too convoluted, isn't it?

Free will is often offered up as the grand solution to the problem of evil. In this scenario, God wanted people to choose him freely so that their love for him might be shown to be sincere. While this seems plausible at first blush, it falls apart under closer inspection. Would the test really have to be so ridiculously stark and monumentally consequential? Why couldn't there be a more graceful way to go about this? Isn't sincere love and trust something that is learned and earned over time? Is it even fair to put the first two freshly minted humans to this test before they even have a chance to understand the world they have been ushered into? Isn't that on the level of condemning a child to capital punishment for tossing his food on the floor after he's been told not to? And then there's a more fundamental question: Is free will really worth the eternal suffering of the majority of humanity? Why would it be? What kind of bizarre calculus could justify this?

START MAKING SENSE

As a human being it is my right to ask these questions. After all, it is my life, my experience, my existential meaning on the line. If I am asked to believe something on pain of death, shouldn't I expect it to make a little more sense? Or is that exactly the reason for the threat? There really doesn't seem to be a good answer to the problem of why a God with all the power and all the love does not interfere when people cry out to him in the midst of abuse, pain, and suffering. At least, why doesn't he interfere just a little bit more? As far as we can tell, he doesn't seem to be doing much of anything.

Or, in the grander scheme, why did he set up a scenario in which we are even asking the question in the first place? We can cover over it with an anecdote about someone who came to God and sees how all their suffering now makes sense. But that is superficial and ignores the other stories that don't end that way. The suicides; the people who became emotionally stunted for their entire unhappy lives; the kids who turned into abusers when they got older. Let me put it this way: If I had the power to stop a guy from beating his kid, and the kid was pleading with me to do so, then I would answer his pleas. Most people would; even people with questionable morals would. Isn't it a sign of incoherence that we have to make excuses for God not interfering in such manifestly unjust situations, particularly when he is asked to do so?

I'm talking as if I'm questioning the actions of an entity called "God" who is presumed to exist, and calling him out as incoherent. I have to admit that even now, as a secular person who knows that this God is an illusion, it still feels just a little bit too incautious and irreverent. It still feels like I should moderate my language and pose my complaints in a more respectful tone, just in case The Being does after all exist. Because if he does, I'm in the deepest of all shit. I don't really believe that he exists, but after thinking of him as real for the greater part of my life, there is a shortcut somewhere in my brain—one last bit of wiring I haven't managed to track down—that makes me feel like I'm criticizing an actual being and not just a bad idea.

> And because at some level I think that You are a real person, one who is both deeply loving and infuriatingly childish, it can be difficult to maintain my objectivity when I talk about this biggest of all Your flaws. Because if You are just a bad idea, then it seems much easier to process all this. People are easily misled, I can say, by their hopes and fears. They come up with wacky explanations and they believe their own silly stories without somehow factoring in that they are just stories they themselves invented. I can view that with equanimity. But if You are a real entity, who both cares and judges on that awesome and terrifying scale, well, in that case it now feels like the right reaction isn't just analysis, but anger and resentment, and maybe even hate. How dare You put us in this insane situation? What were You thinking? The maker does not get to blame his creation for being flawed. *You* came up with this plan, not me. You are the one who sat there in your heavenly place and thought this was all a great idea. I just got born into it and I was ushered into it without any notion about what is going on. And I'm supposed to swallow all this incoherency and just go along with it, or else? Your instructions are confusing, and Your standards inconsistent. And the stakes are completely out of proportion. And if me being pissed off about this means you are going to punish me forever in your torture chamber, if that really is how cruel and absurd reality is, then—even if I end up regretting this after a billion years of torture—then I say, *bring it on*. I'm fed up with being pressured by You and Your followers to adhere to some childish scrawl of a

grand unified theory of life which is so obviously the product of the most thoughtless urges of the human mind. It's time to grow up. Time to exorcise the demons of the mind and take a stand. It may be small and futile, but it's *my* stand, not Yours.

In Jesus name, Amen.

Though I try to make this a completely intellectual assessment, there is clearly more going on here. Deeply held emotions and deeply etched neural pathways conspire to keep me in the fold, projecting on the screen of my mind an anthropomorphic figure that incorporates this bundle of doubt, hope, fear, and occasional clarity. And that projection is God to me. And recognizing that projection as projection is a task that I must return to again and again.

Evangelicals delight in pointing out that atheists are angry at the God they don't believe exists, as if this proves something. They think it means that we are in denial. We know on some deep level, they claim, that God exists and no matter how hard we try to deny his existence, our own words and emotions betray us. But when they do this, they are only showing the rest of us that they have not themselves confronted their own projection. They have just given into and naively swallowed the tale that they have told themselves, hook, line, and sinker. They have lacked the insight to engage in the most important question in all of this: Does this God of yours exist in reality, or does he only exist in your mind? Because I don't question that God exists in my mind. Of that, I'm sure. I talk to him on most days. Well, most *weeks* by now. To simplistically extrapolate what is happening in your brain to what is happening in the real world is one of the most basic errors of thinking.

And aren't these theological responses to "the problem of evil" all post-fact justifications of an untenable position? Isn't the simplest explanation that there is no all-powerful, all-loving deity? All this illustrates what happens when people insist on believing something that clashes so explicitly with experience.

The result is a complicated set of answers that only seems to address the question if one has already accepted the conclusion. Wouldn't it have been better if I had been equipped to respond to this kid in a secular fashion? "Life can really suck," I might have said. "I get that. But you can move on. You can overcome this if you work, if you try. It's hard, but you can do it. I will help you and we have resources." That seems like a pretty good answer to me now. But I couldn't say that back then because I was too busy trying to figure out what went wrong with my theology. It's awkward to say, "I don't know why this God who loves you did not answer your urgent prayers, but he does love you and wants to heal you. You should believe in him and seek him in spite of the lack of evidence." I'm sure that is the prescribed answer, and I'm sure that is what other, more committed, Christians would have said. But I empathized too much with him to feed him that sort of incoherence, and I intuited that he had no motivation to put faith in a baseless answer. And maybe what this anecdote teaches about me is that, when push comes to shove, I've always felt the voice of reason arguing against faith.

CHAPTER 7
YOU WILL BURN IN HELL FOR THIS

We are all so accustomed to the idea of hell that I think we have become immune to the sheer level of viciousness and violence it deploys. Nothing threatens to do more harm to a human being more cruelly than never-ending torture by fire. Sacred depictions of hell in religious art from the medieval and renaissance eras are truly vile and unworthy of a religion that claims to represent a God who is the very definition of love. During this time, it was common practice to place so-called doom walls on the western walls of churches, so that exiting worshipers could be reminded of what was at stake. Typically, these paintings showed Jesus in the center determining the fate of dead humans. Those on his right head off into a blissful and peaceful heavenly place, while those on the left go to hell. It's easier to depict pain and horror than bliss in a painting, and I suppose that is why the hell side tends to be the most graphic. Here we may witness people, typically nude, being dragged off by monstrous demons; tortured, skewered, thrown into fire, and beaten with various tools. Brunelleschi's dome in Florence has a last judgment scene with a band that depicts hell on the bottom. This can be seen very clearly on the trip to the top of the church that uses the old workers' stairways. Particularly striking to me is a demon with extended wings and three large goat heads rising out of the flames. Each head is in the process of devouring a human being. Surely these images packed a punch in a culture with limited access to art, or images of any sort, haunting the dreams and imaginations of the most impressionable.

Medieval and Renaissance depictions of hell are also a poor fit for a contemporary movement like evangelicalism which claims to be pro-life, pro-family, and frets about violence in film and in television. Even if many evangelicals might disavow these sorts of lurid depictions, their dehumanizing scenes are actually faithful portrayals of the idea of hell, in the sense that it's pretty much one of the most horrible things one can imagine. Though the Bible itself contains no details about the daily nature of hellish life, the idea of being punished forever in the "lake of fire" that is described in Revelation is pretty much unsurpassable. Rape me, chop me up into little pieces, quarter me, put me on the rack for a year, pull my intestines out while I'm watching. In a game of would-you-rather, any of these things beats getting burned alive forever. The idea is so completely and utterly over the top that those who don't believe it have a hard time taking it seriously, and also have a hard time understanding just how despicable it is.

Hell is particularly wounding and disturbing to children who, aside from having a very active imagination, also tend to take the claims of adults very seriously—even when they are ludicrous. Fortunately (that might not be the right word here), most children are exposed to hell in the context of a message about salvation. And so they are perhaps not as terrorized by it as they might be otherwise. They, of course, take advantage of their get-out-of-hell-free card, brought to them conveniently by the same company that invented hell[TM], minimizing their terror. But it's not that simple. Not every child is convinced of the efficacy of their salvation, as when, for example, many children continue to pray the prayer of salvation over and over and in different ways just to be sure they did it right. It never ceases to amaze me that adults who "like to work with children" and seem to sincerely have their best interests in mind, will terrorize them with these sorts of religious horrors. And parents who would never allow their children to watch R-rated films, let alone anything in the horror genre, cheerfully send them to Sunday school, vacation Bible school, and Christian summer camps, where they are inducted into the greatest horror story of all time. Hell really is frightening, and real people do live in fear of it, even though it is a complete and total fabrication for which there is not one sliver of evidence other than the writings of some ancient religious authors.

BLASPHEMY AGAINST THE HOLY SPIRIT

When I was about ten years old, I was dutifully reading my Bible and I came across the passage about the sin against the Holy Spirit,

> I tell you the truth, all the sins and blasphemies of men will be forgiven them. But whoever blasphemes against the Holy Spirit will never be forgiven; he is guilty of an eternal sin (Mark 3:28-29).

I was immediately concerned, for even at that young age (already a budding theologian), I immediately realized that this was out of step with the rest of the message of the Bible. A sin that can't be forgiven is extremely intimidating and concerning. I thought I was safe from hell! Now it turns out I can still screw this up? And worse, the sin was absurdly easy to commit. I could change my entire eternal destiny in the next minute if I just said a few words. It was similar to the feeling of standing on a cliff and knowing that a simple twitch of muscles could end my life right then and there. Only the feeling was magnified and even more consequential.

At the time, my family was living in a Spanish-speaking country where they have a different constellation of swear words than Americans. (Yes, I'm now going to teach you how to swear in Spanish.) A few days after reading this passage, with it still weighing heavily on my mind, I was walking down the sidewalk and I passed by some bricklayers who were having trouble with their work. One of them let out a string of obscenities, among them the expletive "I shit on the Holy Spirit." I had never heard that expression before, and I haven't heard anyone say it since. Part of me wonders whether I may have misheard due to my mental state, because it is a very unusual expression (in Spanish, "Me cago en el Espiritu Santo") and a very strange thing to say given the relevant biblical passage. I was of course shocked by the realization that I had just witnessed someone condemn themselves to hell right in front of me. This is exactly what I had feared doing myself. And this guy was leaning into it with gusto. The event was so disturbing that even today, some fifty years later, I still find myself in an emotionally heightened state when describing it, and I still have trouble transcribing the curse without a feeling of unease.

The phrase was stuck in my ten-year-old head and that was the end of me. Because now it wasn't just a matter of knowing that I could, somehow, say something that would land me forever, unforgiven and unforgivable, in hell. Now I had a formula, conveniently provided by the blasphemous bricklayer. And so, intrusive thoughts being what they are, I eventually repeated the phrase in my mind. I couldn't stop myself. It just sprung out of my brain. And then, it kept coming! It was all over. I had the rest of my life to live, but it would always be overshadowed by the knowledge that when I died, an eternity of unmitigated terror awaited me, because I had blasphemed the Holy Spirit.

I moped around the house for several days in a state of genuine mental and emotional distress, and my father finally noticed that something was up. So I confessed my sin. He was very kind and reassured me that I had not, in fact, blasphemed against the Holy Spirit. The way he explained it, the sin of blasphemy against the Holy Spirit involved not just saying some words, but a consistent and determined rejection of him and his entreaties to believe and obey. In other words, it involved what I'm doing now in my rejection of Christianity—but not the involuntary production of intrusive phrases. I'm not sure that explanation really works, since the passage is a response to some "teachers of the law" who claimed that Jesus was casting out demons by the power of the devil. That was the blasphemy, and blasphemy is something you say at a point in time. Like a curse or a swear word. But for a ten-year-old, any adult explanation will do. And so, I was off the hook! I had my life back. A tremendous burden was lifted. And that was the end of the story.

Unfortunately, the exact same scenario would eventually be repeated when I had my own children. Our family was on vacation at a cabin on an island in British Columbia, and my then wife and I suddenly realized that our daughter had been very quiet for several hours. When we asked about it, they[1] were silent. Clearly, they were very upset about something. After attempting to elicit an explanation, we decided to let it rest, in the hope that it would all come out in time. After a couple days of this, during which we were very concerned, with a cloud hanging over our vacation time, my daughter finally spoke to me, late in the night, revealing they were afraid that they might commit blasphemy against the Holy Spirit. They were so upset about it they did not want to utter a single word for fear of saying something that would land them in hell. At the time I was a Bible teacher, and even then I was still bothered by this passage. The explanation my father had given me, which I had since realized is standard fare among evangelicals, did not really work, exegetically speaking. It was a bit of a sore point. I had by then managed to silo off this passage and its claims as just too ridiculous to be taken seriously. It was completely out of step with the rationale of the entire New Testament. The idea that there should be a grand exception to the rule of free forgiveness for all sin just made no sense. And that it would be this particular act was also bizarre. Not mass murder, not rape, not child abuse, but attributing the work of the Holy Spirit to the devil? Really? Why would God or the Holy Spirit care that much about this? Why could you be forgiven for blaspheming God the Father, and Jesus the Son, but not the Holy Spirit? Aren't they the same anyway because of the trinity? Theologians have their explanations, but the Bible itself does not explain it. By this time, in my own mind, I had dismissed the passage as a weird aberration, and I no longer took it seriously. But I couldn't really say that to my daughter, or really to anyone, because it brought up a bigger question: "Wait a minute, Rob. You are saying that you just toss out passages from the Bible because you think they make no sense?" (Well… yes, it turns out.) That's not what good evangelicals do. And it's certainly not what Bible-teaching evangelical leaders do!

But I needed to help my daughter get past this, so I sheepishly gave them the same rationale that my father had given me, even though I didn't think it made any sense. Fortunately, it satisfied them and my daughter was given a new lease on life and their ability to speak was restored. This encounter with the passage was less disturbing than my first one, but I could not help but feel a little bit stupid and cowardly for putting my child in the position of believing something that was so distressing. Why hadn't I learned from my experience and taken steps to avoid this for my own children?

LOVE DOESN'T WIN

Evangelicals have an odd relationship with hell. On one hand, they seem to vehemently believe it. Any evangelical who questions the reality of hell will be ostracized very quickly as Rob

Bell, megachurch pastor and producer of the popular video series NOOMA, found out in 2011 when he claimed, in his book called *Love Wins*, that hell was not forever because God's love would, well, *win* in the end. The response from evangelical thought leaders was swift and clear: that's unbiblical, heretical, and just plain wrong.

On the other hand, evangelicals also prevaricate around the topic. For example, evangelical darling C.S. Lewis, writer of the *Chronicles of Narnia* series, wrote a book called *The Great Divorce* that presented hell as a tawdry town on the edge of heaven. Everyone was free to take the bus to heaven, but most did not want to. So the idea here is that hell is something you choose because of your own petty self-indulgence at the expense of experiencing the liberating glory of God. Delightfully, hell even had a group of theologians! Evangelicals really like this take and they like to put it forward in conversations about hell. It is a far cry from a lake of fire. But it's not really a replacement so much as an excuse to talk about something that sounds a little less horrifying and insane to non-Christians. Similarly, there is the idea that hell is just the place where God's influence is completely absence and so it is bound to be horrible. If you choose not to be with God, it's the only option left. It's not like God *designed* the place to be horrible. That's just what it's bound to become. Another thing that makes some evangelicals squirm is the problem of condemning people to hell who have not had a chance to hear the gospel. It seems that through no fault of their own, they never even had the chance to do the right thing and believe in Jesus. Is it really fair to send them to hell? In cases like this, many evangelicals will just say something like, "I trust God will be fair in that situation." But this problem is actually acute, if you let it percolate: God can't engineer history such that everyone has a chance to hear the gospel? Why on earth not? In short, evangelicals believe in hell—eternal, fiery, inevitable—but they would rather not talk about it unless they have to. And maybe that means they sort of believe it and they sort of don't believe it.

I myself was particularly uncomfortable with a passage at the end of the book of Isaiah that envisions a new heaven and a new earth in which all people bow down to God, and then, after this worship service, they "go out and look upon the dead bodies of those who rebelled against [God]; their worm will not die, nor will their fire be quenched, and they will be loathsome to all mankind" (Isaiah 66:24).

For me the sore point is the idea of gloating over dead bodies. Who would really want to do this? This level of vindictiveness is just too high, even for a sinner like me. I just can't fit that into my brain alongside biblical claims of love, forgiveness, and compassion. It highlights that, ultimately, the message of the Bible remains vicious and violent in spite of or somehow in parallel with its loftier claims about grace, peace, and love.

This Isaiah passage is reiterated by gentle Jesus, meek and mild, when he describes hell as the place where the worm does not die and the fire never goes out (Mark 9:43-48). According to Jesus, any part of your body, be it your eye, your hand, or your foot, that might cause you to sin ought to be amputated if it might land you in hell. And he does have a point when he says that it is better to enter heaven with missing body parts than to go to hell whole. It's unclear in what sense any of this is literal (presumably we get missing body parts back when we go to heaven?), but what is clear is that Jesus thought hell was real and just. He's not questioning the fact of hell, only providing expert advice on how to avoid it. Jesus was not averse to insinuating that his opponents were going to hell (Matthew 23:33), and he thought of himself as the one who would determine the fate of the dead on judgment day by deciding who would go there (Matthew 25:31-33). According to the book of Revelation, Jesus, the lamb of God, will preside over the torture of anyone who takes the mark of the beast. These unfortunate people

"…will be tormented with burning sulfur in the presence of the holy angels and of the Lamb. And the smoke of their torment rises for ever and ever. There is no rest day or night for those who worship the beast and his image, or for anyone who receives the mark of his name" (Revelation 14:10-11).

Did the Bible just say that Jesus, that paragon of compassion, is going to watch with satisfaction as human beings are tortured with burning sulfur—forever? Well, that final detail is a bit unclear. Perhaps he will only watch for a while, but the torture is forever. Or perhaps, as envisioned by Isaiah, he will keep coming back to the spectacle from time to time. This calls to mind the scene in the old film *Dr. Phibes Rises Again*, in which the demented Phibes has a person tortured such that his screams provide an accompaniment to his dinner. But while that sort of behavior is considered highly objectionable when performed by humans, it is apparently praiseworthy when attributed to the divine. The grand climax of all this comes in Revelation 20, where first the devil and his henchmen are thrown into the lake of burning sulfur to be "tormented day and night for ever and ever" (Revelation 20:10). Then, everyone else whose name is not written in the book of life is thrown into that same lake of fire as well.

This is all to say that the strangely vindictive account in Isaiah that describes all the good God-worshipers living it up and looking down in judgment on the mangled, tortured, sulfur-burned sinners is, despite all the talk of grace and forgiveness, nevertheless the most fundamental structure of the biblical narrative in both the Old and the New Testament. "We" are going to live the blessed life while "you" are going to scream in agony. "We" might even stop by and watch the show from time to time.

It seems to me that no grand argument is needed to counter this vision of the future. Once we meditate on the details and implications, it becomes clear that the hell story is simply unworthy of belief. It is just too inhuman. Too absurdly malicious and spiteful. At the same time, it indulges in the worst possible impulse of human nature, that of dividing the world into the sphere of the good and the bad, the *us* and the *them*, but on the grandest of all possible scales. Is it any wonder that Christianity regularly reverts to sectarian violence? Christians are eager to offer up the gospel of grace, forgiveness, and salvation, as if this was the defining feature of their belief system. But this is misleading, and perhaps evangelicals are themselves misled by it, for it all rests on a bed of brutal retribution that does not ultimately solve the existential problems of humanity. Or it only solves them by redefining humanity as "us." This is literally how evangelical theologians set up the categories, stating, based on Ephesians 2, that everyone who is in Christ is part of the new humanity. Those who are not part of the new humanity get tossed into the lake of burning sulfur. And even the forgiveness that is magnanimously offered, by grace to the whole world, was only purchased by means of violence: By the death of Jesus on the cross, which is one of the most degrading forms of execution invented by the ancient world. God, we are told, had to subject his own son to this form of death in order to satisfy his own sense of justice. Well, I suppose we should thank him! But this God person is definitely suffering from some serious mental health issues if that is how he handles conflict. And somehow, after sacrificing his own son, he's *still* filled with wrath and still preparing to dole out savage retribution on the world? Those of us who reject violence as a way of life and as a way to solve problems, and those who would use religion to promote peace and understanding, must reject the eternal sectarianism and endless retribution of the Bible. It solves nothing but only extends the destructiveness of human violence into eternity.

No, Rob Bell, I'm sorry to say that you were wrong. Love does not win in the Christian story.

FOREVER TIMES INFINITY

Another question that must be presented to God and the Bible is why does hell have to be eternal and unmitigated? We've all been burned a few times in our lives and we know how much that hurts. Multiply that by (it sounds childish to say it this way) *infinity*. What kind of reasonable intelligent being would think this is an equitable response to anything? And what kind of being with even a sliver of empathy could sit back and watch that happen forever? Viewed from the perspective of someone in hell for eternity, this life was a flash, a nano-second. Their entire existence involves getting born and going straight to hell and being tortured—without end. That is an afront to justice. It is an afront to humanity. Nothing can justify it. Even Hitler doesn't deserve endless torment. Take every single person Hitler harmed and let them have as long as they want to inflict as much pain on him as they like. Even that will be a non-infinite amount of time. And I suspect many people would choose to inflict no pain at all on Hitler because human beings, on average, are not sadists. Except for the theologians who invented hell. Those guys are another level of sadist.

One common evangelical answer to this is to appeal to God's otherness. His holiness, purity, and elevated sense of justice which operates on a plane we lowly sinners cannot comprehend precisely because we are so marred by sin. Hell becomes a pointer to our deficient moral constitution. The reason we don't understand the ratio of crime to punishment is that we don't truly understand the nature of the crime. So, not only is this a mystery (as we have seen, a common enough ploy among believers of things that cannot be demonstrated), but it is a mystery that we cannot ever hope to understand because we are constitutionally unable to understand it. Isn't that kind of the same thing as saying that something doesn't make sense and never will but you should still believe it?

Another attempt to rationalize the justice of hell is to say that an offense against an eternal being deserves an eternal punishment. This is not something the Bible teaches, but yet another rationalization that is added, like an overlay, to the biblical story in order to make sense of it. The real oddity is that the Bible itself does not offer any such explanations and it is clear biblical authors don't have any problem at all with the idea of sending people to hell. It's really only us modern people who struggle with it because of our rational approach to ethics and justice. We tend to think justice should be equitable. And an eternity of punishment can never be an equitable response to affronts committed by creatures of time, whose lifespans are, the Bible itself tells us, less than a grain of sand in the ocean of God's eternal existence.

THE PSYCHOLOGICAL STRUCTURE OF A METAPHYSICAL SPACE

If my readers are not moved to reject the idea of hell because of a capriciousness and sadism that couldn't possibly be the product of a loving or rational being, perhaps a historical argument will pack a better punch. The idea of hell is manifestly the product of the naïve imagination of ancient peoples.

A fact that is little understood in evangelical circles is that most of the Hebrew Bible (the Old Testament) does not even include any explicit teaching about the afterlife. What we have instead is a place called *sheol*, a netherworld which is mentioned often enough, but never really explained. The reason *sheol* is never explained in the Bible is that it represents a view of the afterlife that was shared by all the cultures of the Ancient Near East. In the same way, a religious writer today does not feel the need to explain the concept of God because everyone has a similar enough definition. This netherworld was thought to be a dark and quiet place, associated with earth, dust, and the underground. It is certainly not what we today think of as heaven, but it's not hell either. As the biblical writer of Ecclesiastes put it, "Whatever your hand finds to do, do it with all your might, for in the grave [*sheol*], where you are going, there is neither working nor planning nor knowledge nor wisdom" (Ecclesiastes 9:10), and Job speaks of a land of gloom and deep shadow (Job 19:21). His meditation on his own mortality must sound strange to any evangelical who is paying attention:

> Remember, O God, that my life is but a breath; my eyes will never see happiness again.
>
> The eye that now sees me will see me no longer; you will look for me, but I will be no more.
>
> As a cloud vanishes and is gone, so he who goes down to the grave does not return.
>
> He will never come to his house again; his place will know him no more (Job 7:7-10).

The ancient Hebrews thought of the afterlife as a sleepy, quiet kind of existence that slowly faded, a rest leading to permanent unconsciousness. When King Saul, contrary to the law of Moses, uses a medium to speak to the recently deceased prophet Samuel, a ghostly figure appears and says, "Why have you disturbed me by bringing me up?" (1 Samuel 28:15). The inhabitants of the netherworld, in fact, were sometimes referred to as shades. That the Hebrew scriptures lack any clear teaching about a permanent, conscious, and eternal afterlife is exemplified in the beliefs of the Sadducees, the priestly class of Jews at the time of Jesus, who were essentially materialistic in their beliefs about the soul. This was because they got their beliefs strictly from the first five books of the Bible, which have nothing explicit to say about the persistence of a soul after death.

Humans have been burying their dead since time immemorial, and so the connection between death and dust, earth, and the underground is natural. In ancient Israel and the surrounding cultures, the dead were buried when there was no other option. But the ideal burial, the one to which everyone aspired, was to be placed in a family burial cave. Typically, the bodies were laid out and allowed to desiccate, and then at a later time the dry dusty remains could be gathered into ossuaries, or sometimes they would simply be set aside in a common pile to make room for more recently deceased loved ones. We can see why it would be natural to think of the afterlife as a dark, quiet place in the earth in which individuality and consciousness slowly fades. This is precisely the process the bodies of the dead underwent, as bodies in a dark, dry, and quiet place slowly lost their uniqueness and faded into the dust of the cave.

The ancients seem to have created a mythological or spiritual place simply by extrapolating from the physical state of human bodies after death. This is why it is often difficult to distinguish between the literal grave in which bodies were laid and the netherworld of shadowy conscious existence in the text of the Bible. They imagine the bodies of their loved ones lying in a quiet cave slowly decomposing while in another parallel space, or a kind of additional layer of reality, the souls of their loved ones are also slowly undergoing a similar fading of consciousness. They don't imagine a zombie-like existence in which consciousness slowly fades from a decomposing corpse. That would be too horrible. But what seems clear is that physical reality functions as a springboard for the imagination, and from there the mind leaps into another sphere, less solid and less rational. But surely this is an odd extrapolation. It's just taking a superficial association and running with it with no critical engagement, seamlessly intertwining the physical, the metaphorical, and the spiritual.

The same question rises here as in the rest of this book: If *sheol* is arguably the product of the ancient imagination's meditation on cave burial sites, why are we treating these ideas as if they are sourced in divine revelation? And why do we treat these ideas as if they describe something real? Here's a really odd situation: ideas from Greek mythology regarding Hades, with the river Styx and the ferryman who must be paid two coins, are treated as quaint old tales, and rightly so. But the myths of the Hebrews are treated as revelation? Why? What reason is there, other than that Christianity is believed by many people and that the Bible has been revered for many centuries? That something has been believed is no good reason, in itself, to continue believing it. The Old Testament does not even attempt to place beliefs about the afterlife in the mouth of God. Rather, it simply assumes that what everyone else in the Ancient Near East believed about the afterlife is factual, and the source of those assumptions seems to lie in the ancient imagination.

A typical evangelical answer to this sort of challenge is to claim that just because something in the Bible has parallels in other ancient cultures and religious, it doesn't necessarily mean it's not divine revelation. God could have revealed it to other people too, but the Bible is the clearest revelation. Or God could have used the historical evolution of an idea to reveal it to humanity. These sorts of justifications can never be falsified because, of course, it's all within the realm of possibility given a Christian set of premises. But they hardly rise to the level of any kind of evidence. They are just hypothesis, explanations, and stories. Evidence of supernatural provenance is here, as also in the case of miracles, and in the case of God's purported supervision of our lives, nonexistent. All we have is the affirmation that something which can be shown to be sourced in the human mind is supposedly divine. And this is itself essentially the same kind of intermingling of physical and mental spaces, in which the imaginary becomes the real: The mind thought it, but it came from God.

Similarly, the fact that bodies are often buried and decompose in the ground (or in a burial cave) leaving dust in their place, led to thinking that the human body must be made primarily of dust, or have come from dirt. In fact, it is not true at all that we come from dust. It only seems like we do because once everything that makes a body is subtracted you are left with what was already there in the ground, or cave, where the body was laid. Even an ancient observer might have noted that human bodies come from other human bodies, not from dirt. But the physical process of decomposition became an observation that led to a fact, which even made it into the creation story with its claim that God made the first man out of dust and the poetic notion, also found in the Bible, that we came from dust and will return to dust (Genesis 3:19). This is how superficial associations become theology.

As the centuries passed, ideas about the afterlife evolved. This can be seen in non-canonical Hebrew writings like, for example, the book of Enoch, in which *sheol* was divided into four different chambers—three for the unrighteous and one for the righteous (Enoch 22:3, 9). Later it was simplified to two, as can be seen in the story of the Rich Man and Lazarus in the New Testament. In this story, a poor man, Lazarus, dies and passes his time in a cool and relaxing place called "Abraham's bosom," while a rich man who also dies finds himself in hades, which is the Greek term the New Testament uses for *sheol*. The rich man begs for just a drop of water from Lazarus, but this is unfortunately not possible because of a great divide between them.

In the intertestamental period, and later in the New Testament, *sheol* (or hades) and the bosom of Abraham are not seen as the permanent abode of the dead. Rather, they become holding tanks for both parties as they await the judgment day.

This brings us to Gehenna, which in the New Testament describes the final and eternal, to say nothing of infernal, destiny of the devil, his demons, and all damned humans. When Jesus talks about hell, as we saw earlier in this chapter, he's talking about Gehenna, not *sheol*/hades. This is another spiritual concept with a metaphorical origin. The word "Gehenna" comes from the Hinnom valley on the south side of

Jerusalem, though the precise location given that name in ancient times is debated. *Gehinnom* literally means "valley of Hinnom" in Hebrew and our English Gehenna reflects the Greek transliteration. The valley of Hinnom was famously used in ancient times to offer sacrifices to foreign gods, including human sacrifice. Because of this it was subjected to intense invective, with Jeremiah calling it the valley of slaughter (7:32). It is probably also the valley of dead bodies envisioned in the Isaiah 66 passage, mentioned above, that the righteous look down on, conveniently, from the heights of the city walls. Isaiah also calls out Topheth, the place in the valley used for human sacrifice:

> Its fire pit has been made deep and wide,
> > with an abundance of fire and wood;
> > the breath of the Lord,
> > like a stream of burning sulfur,
> > sets it ablaze (Isaiah 30:33).

Later extra-biblical references to a valley, a pit, or an abyss of judgment should probably also be connected to this valley of Hinnom, as for example,

> And I looked and turned to another part of the earth, and saw there a deep valley with burning fire. And they brought the kings and the mighty, and began to cast them into this deep valley (Enoch 54:1-2).[2]

Fire and sulfur also figure prominently in the brief mentions of the lake of fire, which surely also draws inspiration from this hellish valley.

But we must ask, what came first, the word of God from on high describing hell as something that can be illustrated by the valley of Hinnom, or did the valley of Hinnom evolve over the years in concert with changing ideas about the afterlife to become the full-fledged concept of hell that gives us all nightmares today? Historically speaking, it seems undeniable that the concept evolved. And isn't that evolution of ideas another case of the transmogrification of a superficial association into a metaphor and then into a spiritual and theological truth? People today ask whether hell might be the caldera of a volcano, or where else it might be. The wisest biblical interpreters tell us that it's not clear where hell is! Of course we don't know where (the) hell (it) is. This is because it is located in an impossible metaphorical space, in the imagination, in a dreamlike plane where the physical world of phenomena shifts into the phantasmagorical world of emotionally driven associations. A valley of evil deeds seems dark and foreboding and it transforms into a valley of vengeance, which then transforms into a metaphor of a greater judgment, which then, with the passing of time and the addition of more assumptions and associations, becomes an almost palpable reality that enslaves the mind.

Even the descriptions of the punishments of hell occupy this strange space. Humans are conceived of as dying and going to some non-physical space where they nevertheless experience enjoyments or suffering, like being hot or thirsty, that can only be experienced by physical bodies. How would a soul be thirsty? Thirst comes from lack of water, a chemical element that spirits do not use or need, at least as far as I can tell. By what rationale could a soul experience thirst or be satiated by drinking water, as envisioned in the story of Lazarus and the rich man? On the day of judgment, according to the Bible, all bodies are resurrected, which is to say that people are given bodies again. And some of these bodies are tossed into an eternal fire. The fire is eternal, and this is taken to imply that the suffering in the fire is also eternal. But what sort of body can endure this sort of eternal destruction? The idea itself is contradictory. Destruction means an undoing and an end of things. How can ending be eternal? How can fire forever consume a body? The physics are comically wrong. And if there are no physics involved, since it is spiritual, why are we talking about bodies and fire (chemistry)? The reason that this lack of rationality does not bother those who accept the reality of hell is that hell is not a rational place but, again, a mental place that arises from the combination of free associations surrounding the terror of death, the shame of guilt, and the desire for retribution. Obviously, a human body that is tossed into a lake of fire will be consumed in a matter of minutes, if not seconds.

Theologians are bound to explain this all away by asserting that when the dead are raised again, they are given bodies fit for experiencing all the horrors of fire without being consumed by it. I've heard this one myself. God's second great act of human creation. He's so angry at his production that he lets it die and then brings it back to life especially engineered to survive in a lake of fire forever. This would involve an incredible feat of spiritual/biological engineering in which one makes an indestructible body but leaves in the useless pain receptors. Well, of course, the God of our mind can do anything. But that doesn't mean we should let him.

CHAPTER 8
THE MESSIAH WHO DOESN'T SHOW UP

EMMANUEL

The New Testament posits itself as a solution to the problem of the Old Testament. When Jesus appears on the scene in the pages of the Gospels it is a new day and God is working in a new and more powerful way. Gone is the blessings/curses paradigm. Enter a new era of grace. Now you just have to believe in Jesus to receive God's blessing. Obedience is highly recommended and expected, but the thing that saves you from being cursed and allows you to enter the blessed state is grace. The New Testament also solves, at least rhetorically, the problem of God not showing up. In fact, it presents itself as the great and final moment, the climax, the fulfillment of centuries of longing and doubt. In Matthew 1, which in most printed Bibles is literally the first page of the New Testament, we find this prominent claim, which sets the frame for the rest of the story:

> All this took place to fulfill what the Lord had said through the prophet: "The virgin will be with child and will give birth to a

son, and they will call him Immanuel"—which means, "God with us." (Matthew 1:22-23).

The narrative of the life and ministry of Jesus, as seen in the Gospels, plays the same role in the New Testament as the exodus narrative does in the Old. The Jesus narrative is the foundation for all that follows in the rest of the New Testament. And just as in the case of the exodus narrative, the Jesus narrative is also thick with supernaturalism, with "God among us." Jesus commands demons, heals people, sometimes just by a touch, and makes blind people see. He walks on the water and calms storms, harkening back to the parting of the sea in Exodus. Jesus feeds crowds of people miraculously, just like God did in the wilderness. He turns water into wine and raises people from the dead. Not to mention the climax of the story, where he himself is resurrected after being crucified. On seeing the raised Jesus for himself, the disciple Thomas declares, "My Lord and my God" (John 20:28), and according to the Apostle Paul, the resurrection is the one act that shows incontrovertibly that Jesus is the Son of God (Romans 1:4).

But as we saw in chapter 2, where we discussed the second coming of Jesus, the expectation in the New Testament is that this is all coming to a head very soon with the supernatural intrusion of the kingdom of God and the end of the world as we know it. That is the rational conclusion of the narrative, and it seems to be what Jesus and his early followers expected. Unfortunately, it did not happen. And in its place, we were granted the gift of a future return in glory that recedes at about the same pace as the historical progress of time itself. Always barely out of reach, but near to those who have the eyes of faith. Just as in the exodus narrative, the explicitly miraculous accounts of the gospels fade away rather quickly. The book of Acts, detailing the spread of Christianity after the death of Jesus, includes some miracles, but the focus shifts away from the explicitly supernatural to the more mundane act of preaching and making converts. After Acts, the rest of the New Testament turns into a long, and sometimes difficult to follow, theological disputation with Revelation serving as a bookend. And then, moving forward through history, the miraculous takes a back seat to Christianity as a magisterial religion—Christianity as a bureaucracy that represents God on earth through its authoritative truth claims, not so much because of its visible miraculous power.

Which is to say that it all kind of fizzles, as far as the miraculous is concerned. As with the exodus narrative, the Jesus narrative presents a compelling supernatural tale which subsequent adherents work hard at reproducing but which never materializes.

THE MIRACLE-FILLED LIFE

But Jesus did seem to think his own followers would have the same kind of access to God's explicitly supernatural power that he did. As he says in the gospel of John,

> I tell you the truth, anyone who has faith in me will do what I have been doing. He will do even greater things than these, because I am going to the Father. And I will do whatever you ask in my name, so that the Son may bring glory to the Father. You may ask me for anything in my name, and I will do it (John 14:12-14).

And when he sends out his disciples to preach the gospel in Matthew, he instructs them, "as you go, preach this message: 'The kingdom of heaven is near.' Heal the sick, raise the dead, cleanse those who have leprosy, drive out demons" (Matthew 10:7-8). And they do exactly that in the narrative, setting up the expectation that anyone who is a disciple of Jesus should expect to do similar things.

A well-known and much used passage in the book of

Ephesians teaches that prophecy, which involves predictive and revelatory pronouncements from God, ought to be part of the regular experience of believers (Ephesians 4:11-12). Another passage claims that God gives at least some people miraculous power through the "gifts of the Spirit."

> To one there is given through the Spirit the message of wisdom, to another the message of knowledge by means of the same Spirit, to another faith by the same Spirit, to another gifts of healing by that one Spirit, to another miraculous powers, to another prophecy, to another distinguishing between spirits, to another speaking in different kinds of tongues, and to still another the interpretation of tongues (1 Corinthians 12:8-10).

My favorite passage in the category of "you will also be able to do miracles" is the cursing of the fig tree. Here Jesus comes upon a fig tree that does not have any edible figs. Since he is hungry, he curses it. Then, the next day, when he and his disciples pass by the same place, they find that the tree has withered up. This turns into a lesson on faith, with Jesus telling the disciples that if they believe, they will be able to do things like that themselves, including telling a mountain to throw itself in the sea. "Whatever you ask for in prayer," says Jesus. "Believe that you have received it, and it will be yours" (Mark 11:12-14, 20-25).

The idea that followers of Jesus will be able to heal and be healed by divine power, in continuity with the ministry of Jesus, is also present in the New Testament. In the book of James we have a very specific procedure that, it is claimed, will bring about healing:

> Is any one of you sick? He should call the elders of the church to pray over him and anoint him with oil in the name of the Lord. And the prayer offered in faith will make the sick person well; the Lord will raise him up (James 5:14-15).

This is a surprisingly matter-of-fact statement that just rolls off the page as though it's just a few verses like all the other ones about how to be a good Christian. But let's not miss the claim: You can get healed, presumably from any ailment or disease whatsoever, simply by getting anointed with oil and having some church elders pray for you. Fantastic! Where do I sign up?

IT'S STILL YOUR FAULT

But Christians don't really heal the sick by oil anointings and prayer, nor do they raise the dead or control the weather. To say nothing of moving mountains via voice command. I myself was anointed and prayed for because of a life-threatening medical condition, and nothing came of it. This was just another case of God not showing up. Fortunately, I had secular, scientific medicine to fall back on, and it has kept me alive and ticking quite well for some 55 years. Given there are about 2.3 billion Christians in the world today, we would surely have no diseases at all by now and no need for doctors or medicine if Christian miraculous healing worked. And as for raising the dead, well, I suppose the expectation in the Bible was never that every single dead person ought to undergo that procedure. But still, the text would lead us to hope for a few more instances of resurrection than the current count, which is right around zero. As glorious as all the supernatural powers promised in the New Testament sound, it's just more of the same: intoxicating promises and enthralling miraculous stories that capture the religious imagination, but which in the end don't go anywhere. Those who find the narrative convincing end up chasing the promise of glory for the rest of their lives.

In spite of all the grace poured out in the New Testament, there is one thing that doesn't change. When miracles don't work, when God doesn't show up, it's still your fault. Just like when the blessing didn't come in the Old Testament, you had no one to blame but yourself. This will always be the case so long as miracles are not real and the miraculous promises of Scripture are empty. Because when the much-vaunted miracles don't happen, an explanation must be given. An apologia must be put forward. Someone must be blamed, and it won't be God. That leaves *you*. You, the believer, are the one who gets thrown under the miracle bus.

The *out*, or the apologia—the excuse, some might say—is lack of faith. You also might be asking for the wrong thing, which is itself a kind of lack of faith or a spiritual defect. And this *out* is included or implied in almost every formula or promise, like fine print: "You will be able to do amazing miracles with the power of God!"[1] In the James passage there is the little phrase, "the prayer offered in faith." The implication is that the miraculous power might not manifest itself if you or the people praying don't believe enough.

- Can't move mountains into the sea? It's because you doubted in your heart (Mark 11:23).
- You asked for something, but you didn't get it? Ah, but did you really ask "in my name" and to "glorify the father" (John 14:12-14)? Or maybe you are just being selfish (James 4:3).
- Did you try to cast out a demon and he didn't leave? Maybe you didn't pray hard enough (Mark 9:29) or you lacked faith (Matthew 17:20).
- Are miracles not happening in your church, city, or country? You all, of course, lack faith (Matthew 13:58).
- But also, maybe you didn't confess your sins (James 5:16).

But faith is even more difficult to quantify than obedience to the laws of Moses. How do you measure faith? How do you know when you have enough? And how do you add to it if you need more? And why is it that everyone is so bad at faith? Interestingly, faith works just fine when the thing believed in is unverifiable. When people say they believe in Jesus for salvation, no one questions the effectiveness of their faith. If you say you believe, Christians congratulate you and assume you got saved. See—faith is easy! But of course, there is no observable evidence that anything has happened at all in the spiritual realm, nor can we even verify if there is such a thing as the spiritual realm. But when it comes to doing miracles in the external, physical, and verifiable world that we all inhabit, suddenly faith is really hard, and it appears almost no one can do it! Isn't this all just another version of the apologia? The grand vision of the miraculous life is so compelling that people believe it. Then they go about frantically building a worldview that supports the grand vision in the face of a lived experience that calls it into question.

And if the problem is your motivations, how do you quantify *that*? Motivations are famously difficult to sort out, especially if the thing we are asking for benefits us. And, come to think of it, are we even allowed to ask for ourselves? Wouldn't that be selfish? That's a hard one, given that the vast majority of miracle requests involve things that benefit the requester.

There is one other exculpatory factor as well, but this one is not found in the pages of the New Testament. This is an excuse offered up by believers, namely, that the miracle request might not fit God's plan for our life, for the life of someone else, or for the world. This idea introduces some oddities, as when, for example, evangelicals use the phrasing "if it is your will." As in, "Lord, we ask that you heal little Andrea's pancreatic cancer if it is your will." It also raises the more fundamental question of why people should even bother to ask God for anything if God has a plan for it all, and that plan has got to be far smarter, more loving, and caring than anything we could ever come up with. And what are the chances our requests don't cross paths with his grand scheme? Very small, surely. Some Christians acknowledge this and just say that God inspires us to pray for what he already decided he was going to do. The nice thing about appealing to the mysteries of God's will is that it softens the New Testament's harsher approach in which it is always your own fault if you can't pull off the miraculous.

The net effect of all these qualifiers is that they nicely protect the idea of the miraculous from the less than supernatural reality of life on the ground here on planet earth. You can always blame something other than God, his lack of care, his lack of action, or his lack of existence. But at what cost? In order to believe in the supernatural, we are forced to view ourselves as weak, faithless, selfish, and incapable of charting our own course in the universe. Sounds like a raw deal to me.

WHO NEEDS MIRACLES ANYWAY?

Evangelicalism has two main flavors, charismatic and non-charismatic. In the first flavor, there is a great deal of emphasis on the miraculous in daily life and in the church services themselves. These are the photo-op evangelicals, who raise their hands in praise while tears stream down their faces. All the most popular "miracle workers" are charismatics. In these churches almost every service has a lengthy prayer and healing time, typically towards the end, where people come forward with all sorts of prayer requests: anything from emotional support to healing for cancer. The preachers who lead these meetings tend to pray authoritatively ("We command this cancer in the name of Jesus to *leave*!") and at great length over their parishioners, seemingly contradicting Jesus' teaching that prayers are not made any more efficacious because of their many words. I can't help but to imagine God up in heaven saying, "Ok, ok, I heard you the first time!"

The non-charismatics, on the other hand, are more staid and rational. Think of Billy Graham. Billy didn't do any miracles. He just preached the gospel. In these churches people do still believe in the miraculous, but it is more subtle. There is the miracle of changed hearts or the miracle of God working everything out for the best. These people do also pray for healing and other miracles. The centerpiece of services in the non-charismatic churches is the sermon, where Scripture is explained and applied to life. Dancing, weeping, and supernatural acts that happen right before your eyes don't tend to be encouraged in such churches. In the most extreme case, some Christians don't even believe that miracles happen anymore. This theological doctrine is called cessationism, meaning the miraculous gifts mentioned in the New Testament, like miraculous healing and prophecy, are no longer active in the world. They have ceased. The rationale is that once God provided the Bible there was no further need for miracles. Who needs miracles now that you have the Truth? Well, some of us wouldn't be averse to experiencing a taste of the supernatural, but okay. Whether it is planned or not, the effect of cessationism is to conveniently put miraculous claims beyond the prying eyes of critical enquiry. No one can go back two thousand years and look closely at all the miracles in the Bible, and no one can look at miracles today because they don't happen anymore.

It will come as no surprise that charismatics and cessationists don't get along very well. In fact, they love to criticize each other. Charismatics tend to preach a lot, and cessationists tend to write densely argued books. Combining their critiques of each other can be enlightening. The cessationist accuses the charismatic of being too credulous and agrees with a skeptical analysis of purported miracles: hype and psychology turns out to be a better explanation of the phenomena than God's power. So this is a case of Christians themselves critiquing the supernatural. But they don't seem to realize that once they are done criticizing the charismatics, there isn't much left to work with. Charismatics, on the other hand, accuse the cessationists of being too rational. And they have a point. If you are going to be a supernaturalist and follow a guy who did plenty of miracles, it seems like miracles ought to be par for the course. And, as I've documented above, the idea that Christians should expect to experience the supernatural is found in the pages of Scripture. If you combine these two critiques, what you get is this:

1. To be authentic to the Jesus narrative you should expect to experience the supernatural in ways that are similar to what the Bible describes. But the only way you can do that is by indulging in credulity and suppressing rationality.
2. To engage in a more credible embodiment of the Jesus narrative, you have to suppress the idea that Jesus' followers should experience the supernatural world that is found in the gospels. But how credible is a supernatural religion that has no miracles, and why would anyone believe it?

And I have to wonder if the Christianity of the cessationists is more of a mind game, where even the miracles of the past are just pieces of the puzzle that is their doctrine. And why would this even come about, that a large subsection of a miraculous religion stopped believing in miraculous activity? Perhaps the reason is that deep down they are not entirely convinced themselves that miracles are real, and so they have invented a miracle-less religion.

CHAPTER 9
MIRACLES AND NOISE

MY FIRST HEALING CAMPAIGN

Once, when I was a guest speaker at a charismatic church, I was asked to lead the healing service after my message. I went along with it, but on the inside I was not happy. I had not prepared for it, and it was not my kind of ministry. But it can be hard to say "no" in situations like that. People were particularly interested in having me pray for a young girl, perhaps six or seven years old, who had a headache. But I was worried. What if her headache was something serious? What if I prayed and nothing happened? What was I supposed to do then? Just keep praying? It's one thing to pray for God to work something out in the future or to heal a vague ailment. But here's a very specific situation: I have a headache. Please make it stop.

So I prayed.

I struggled to imitate healing prayers I had heard in the past, I tried to be authoritative without sounding like I was just making things up, and I sincerely hoped that God would answer. When I was done, I asked the girl how she felt. And to my surprise, she said she felt better. I also felt suddenly better!

What a relief on so many different levels: While I was genuinely happy that she was no longer suffering, I was also off the hook for doing something about her health. And finally, and perhaps most importantly, I had literally witnessed a miracle! I had basically been the agent of the miracle. God did it, obviously, but I was the one who asked, and it really happened! That felt tremendous. It was vindicating. See? Miracles *do* happen.

On the way home from the meeting, the local pastor, who knew I was not used to doing that sort of thing, joked that it was my first healing campaign. But I didn't go on to do any more healings. Healing was cool, I thought, but I'm an intellectual, first and foremost. I believed my role in the church was to teach. It took several years for this experience to percolate in my brain. As I looked back I realized that for all I knew that little girl did not get better. For all I knew, she had a brain tumor, still felt a headache, and was dead within a few months. Or it might have been a more benign headache, but still no healing happened. Imagine the pressure that a little six-year-old kid will be bound to feel when adults come around her, pray authoritatively, and then ask if she feels better—with the clear implication that she's supposed feel better now. She may very well pick up on all the cues and say that the headache is gone when it isn't. On the other hand, it might have been a headache caused by stress, and having everyone come around her and make her the focus of attention produced an emotional high which caused the symptoms of stress to fade. Looking back now, I have to confess I have no idea what happened that day, and I can't say with any certainty whether or not a miracle took place.

TOO MUCH NOISE

And this is the problem with all miracles. Sorting out the supernatural causes, if there be any, from the natural ones is extremely difficult. If it can even be done at all. To make matters worse, believers, in their rush to confirm the miraculous, regularly trample the distinction—like a herd of elephants.

Where miracles are reported, we are typically dealing with people who already believe in the supernatural, so they are more likely to identify something as "unexplainable" and to attribute it to the supernatural. Religious people want miracles. As we have already seen, the desire to see God at work in one's life is a key component of Christian spirituality. So, a systematic and careful evaluation of all the factors that are at work is not the first thing on people's minds when they identify a possible miracle. Rather, an unexplainable event feels more like an expectation fulfilled. Believers already believe. They are over that fence. They are not primed to be skeptical or to ask probing questions. And reports of miracles mostly come to the rest of us from these noncritical sources.

The majority of those who experience purported miracles are lay people. These folks are not necessarily equipped with a sophisticated enough understanding of how the material world works in order to know all the possible physical causes that might explain a particular phenomenon, be they medical, psychological, sociological, or related to any other field of study. They are just dealing with life. All they know is that they prayed for something they really needed to happen and then it happened, or they were suddenly confronted with a unique experience that they could not explain.

There is the problem of coincidence and luck. If you predict the toss of a coin, you will be right about 50% of the time. If you pray for something you want, it will come about a certain percentage of the time, even in a materialistic, godless universe. If you pray for healing, you will get better a certain percentage of the time. We all know the body can heal itself. But if you prayed for it, "Lo! It's a miracle!" If the doctor tells you that you are going to die in three months, he will be wrong a certain percentage of the time, maybe even because of a misdiagnosis. If everyone prayed for healing every single time they were sick, a certain percentage of prayers would seem to have been answered. But in fact, this would have been just the natural course of things. This alone makes it extremely easy to believe in miracles if one is predisposed to belief in them. But there's more: We also tend to remember successes and forget failures. So we are bound to put great stock in the times we sought a miracle and got it, and we are bound to forget all the times we asked and we didn't receive. In any case, the reality of luck and coincidence has to be factored into any report of a miracle, but often it is not.

How do we isolate the purported supernatural causes from the material causes? When a person asks for divine intervention, they are typically doing many other things as well, like talking to their friends and loved ones about their problems, asking fellow believers to pray for them, taking medicine, trying to get loans, or whatever the situation calls for. When people really want something, they throw everything at it. So, was it really the prayer that brought about the desired outcome, or was it the other things the praying person did? All these things are sources of noise and imprecision. I'm not saying they can't be overcome, but that they are not usually overcome, and so people who believe in the supernatural come away with the impression that there has been a supernatural event in their lives when the evidence isn't so decisive as it seems. Believers are also happy to give credit to God even where there are multiple possible causes for the outcome. This is because they already believe that God is doing things, and they are happy to attribute even the secondary causes to him. Here's a hypothetical example of how this could go:

> "I prayed because I was going to get kicked out of my apartment and I didn't have rent money. Then I went to my friend who owed me $500 and it just so happened that he had just received money from a settlement, and he was able to pay me, and I didn't lose my apartment. God made it all work out."

This does not remotely count as evidence for God's intervention or of the supernatural. It is evidence of a motivated person doing what it takes to get by in the world and a little bit of good timing. Similarly, there was the time in my life when the water heater broke down, yes, you guessed it, in the middle of winter. My then wife mentioned this as a prayer request in a prayer meeting and after praying about it, the group came together and gave us the funds that we needed to buy a new one. While this was very generous of them and we were thankful for it, I was not tempted to chalk it up as a miracle.

Many miraculous claims are surrounded by hype and technique. For example, people can only get healed in a highly charged meeting where they must come forward before a pumped-up audience who wants to see a miracle, and incredible peer pressure is at work. Faith healers purposefully craft these miracle events because they apply the desired psychological pressures and group dynamics that lead to the miracle. Said another way, why don't faith healers have office hours, like regular doctors? Obviously because there is no spectacle. These spectacles are a world unto themselves. The only thing that matters in these meetings is that someone have a satisfying public reaction to the miracle worker. There is no need to verify the miracle afterwards, and once the recipient is off the stage, it doesn't matter what they say or do or feel because they have already fulfilled their part in the finely crafted "supernatural" event. Nothing about these sorts of events is even remotely credible. Every single part can be subjected to critical scrutiny and found wanting.

We humans perpetually underestimate the capacity other humans have for deception, both conscious and unconscious. I always laugh when someone describes an unlikely event reported by a third party, and after I express skepticism, they say something like this: "Well, you aren't saying they are *lying,* are you?" As though this is absurd and completely unwarranted. But it *is* a possibility. Even an upright, ethical person can stretch the truth or leave out significant details, while convincing themselves they are being truthful. I have even seen confessions by Christians, admitting that they fabricated miracles to get attention. But we seem to have built-in biases that keep us from being overly skeptical in certain situations: If we know the person, if they have a reputation in our circles, or if they seem sincere. Another funny response is to say something like this: "Well, I understand that people do sometimes lie, but no one would lie about something like *this*." If you ever think this or something like it, beware, because you are probably about to get conned. It is exactly these sorts of sensibilities that con artists take advantage of. "No one would steal money from an old lady who is in the hospital!" So, you trust. And they steal your money. Whatever it is you think people would probably never do, there is someone out there doing it right now. Including miracle workers who are just manipulating people because it's easy money, and storytellers who make up stories about divine intervention because they like the attention.

Additionally, though, people can be self-deceived. They can talk themselves into believing something really happened when it didn't. Or the details about what happened can slowly grow such that eventually you really do have a lie, but it is sincerely believed. The reward system is hugely influential. People can get tremendous meaning from being the one to whom something amazing happened. It takes a lot of wisdom and attention to detail to sort through all these issues. Attention to detail and wisdom are not always front and center in situations where a miracle is supposed to have occurred.

The part played by psychosomatic issues. There is such a thing as psychosomatic illnesses. They can come in the form of imagined ailments which are the product of worry or of obsessing over certain bodily sensations. But people also experience real bodily pain because of their mental state. Even true pain, like a bad knee, headaches, and many other things, can result from chronic frustration, sadness, fear, and worry. And if a charismatic individual enters the life of someone who is weighed down by stress and psychosomatic symptoms, and this individual manages to authoritatively combine all the deeply held beliefs of the afflicted person to declare, perhaps in the presence of others, that the sufferer is healed, this can cut through psychosomatic issues and produce a healing. But perhaps only for so long as the impression lasts.

Psychosomatic issues also manifest in ways that illustrate just how much our mental models and presuppositions can produce physical responses. One fascinating example is the "no-touch knockout" in martial arts, whereby some martial arts instructors claim to have mastered the technique of knocking a person out without touching them. The practitioner typically motions with his hands and his opponent, or many opponents, will just fall over, apparently by the force of the blow. A skeptic might say that everyone is just faking it. However, this does not seem to be the case. It seems that everyone involved really thinks the no-touch knockout works. For further evidence, you can attend a charismatic church or watch videos of Benny Hinn online. Like the no-touch knockout black belt, these preachers also blow people over, sometimes with a light touch, and other times with no touch at all. They call it being slain in the spirit. People in the congregation who are looking for a blessing will line up on stage and fall over on queue when the preacher motions to them in one way or another.

It seems difficult to claim that all these participants are consciously colluding in this, and so the demonstrations seem to have a certain legitimacy to them, particularly if one is already predisposed to give them credence. The preacher is perceived to be in command of the power of God. He actually blows people over with it! But the important point here is that there are not just two options, either it is real or it is faked. There is a third option: It is not real, but it is not faked either. Those involved in the event really do believe it is legitimate because they are caught up in the psychological and social forces at work. This was vividly demonstrated in the case of Japanese martial arts master Yanagi Ryuken who was so convinced of his own powers that he offered five thousand dollars to anyone who could withstand his no-touch knockout. A journalist schooled in martial arts accepted the challenge and easily defeated him (the fight can be seen online). And we ask, "how could someone have become so convinced of his own fake powers as to allow them to be challenged so openly?" We must adjust our thinking. There are many charlatans, but there are also many people who passionately believe false and irrational things and convince others of them as well. In fact, this might be the more common scenario.

The one-step-removed factor. In modern churches one may observe an interesting recurring theme when preachers, and then lay people in conversation, relate incredible miracles that have occurred elsewhere in the world, including people being raised from the dead. This is so common that there is a perception among many Christians that miracles don't happen here in "the West" because we are too skeptical. Miracles are perceived to happen only in other, poorer parts of the world where people are more open to spiritual reality and where God can work miracles.

But step back for a moment and consider the alternative: What if there are other reasons that miracles always happen somewhere else? First, these distant miracle reports typically come from places where people are poor and uneducated. Perhaps they are more easily convinced than educated Westerners that a miracle has occurred, perhaps they have less access to sophisticated medical assessments, perhaps they themselves have a miraculous worldview that influences their own interpretation of events. Second, the biases of the *listeners* make the report of a miracle more believable. In fact, these Western listeners not only think God does miracles, but they are eager to see that sort of thing happen to them. They *want* to believe the report. Third, distance and ambiguity of details cover over any problems. The listener knows nothing about the context, the community, or the longevity of the miracle. And so, perhaps the reason that miracles always seem to happen somewhere else is that somewhere else is the only place they *can* happen. Right here receives too much scrutiny and the result is that we see the "miracle" for what it is: a non-miracle. It is easy to believe a report about a distant miracle without engaging in critical thinking if we are already predisposed to believe in miracles and we already wish they happened more often.

It seems God only does certain kinds of miracles. These are typically hidden in the sense that the actual miraculous action takes place *incognito*, and all we see is the result. This is particularly notable with medical issues, where miracles involve God healing a pain, on the say-so of the subject—just like in my healing campaign. No one knows what changed in their body. Or, a doctor provides a concerning diagnosis, but after another test (and prayer), the diagnosis is reversed. We almost never get the claim that people literally observed unexplainable phenomena. For example, in the Bible there is the parting of the Red Sea, or the time when Joshua made the day longer so the Israelites could win a battle, or in the ministry of Jesus where a man's shriveled hand was cured in the sight of everyone. In these cases, everyone supposedly witnessed a supernatural event. You could have observed it with your friend and you could have both looked at each other in amazement and known that you were witnessing something unexplainable happening right before your eyes. Like in the movies. These overtly miraculous things happen in the Bible, but in modern religious life miracles have a decidedly more subtle manifestation. You won't hear about, and believers won't expect, straight-out miraculous events like a severed foot growing back before your eyes, a person levitating in front of a group of people, or a rash healing up in seconds. And just forget about walking on water, immediate calming of storms, and bringing people who are really dead back to life. Believers don't expect these things and they don't ask God for them. But why? If miracles are real, then why is the typical miracle always the subtle type, where the miraculous action is hidden and unobservable? And these days, when practically every square foot of the world is being recorded by someone's phone, why don't we have copious video footage of overt miraculous events? It's hard to avoid the conclusion that miracle action is usually hidden because miracle action only exists in the mind.

HOW TO HANDLE MIRACLE FAILS

The points above are all factors which make it hard to decide whether a purported miracle really was a miracle. But there are also issues on the flipside which mitigate against miracle fails. These are patterned responses that are brought out when one thinks a miracle should have happened but it doesn't. These add even more noise to the question of the existence of miracles, because miracle fails can't be used as evidence against miracles. This should by now sound familiar: When it comes to faith, things that work point to God. But things that don't work, don't count.

The presence of principles which do not allow for negation. In other words, sophistry when it comes to talking about the supernatural. What I mean are statements like the popular adage that can be heard in endless sermons and devotional books: God always answers prayer. Sometimes he says yes, sometimes he says no, and other times he says wait.

This statement is finely crafted to ensure that prayer is never placed under critical scrutiny by those who pray, and it also takes full advantage of the already noted dynamics of chance and luck. Let's imagine for the sake of the argument that there is no God. This spiritual sounding adage would still maintain the faith of the credulous, for sometimes a prayer would be answered by mere coincidence or by the actual effort of the praying person. Other times, prayer for a request would be roundly rejected, as for example, where one prays for a dream job and the company goes bankrupt. At other times, the desired thing might happen in the future, or the praying person can comfort themselves with the idea that this may be so. And if the prayed-for event does happen in the future, the praying person will of course attribute it to God.

Miracle victim blaming. We've already discussed this in the last chapter, so I'll just briefly reiterate the fact that when miracles fail to materialize, the Bible itself provides us with rationales that safeguard the miraculous from criticism: It's the miracle requester's fault. They either lacked faith, or their motivations were not pure enough. Possibly, also, it was just a dumb human idea that conflicted with God's much better plan.

Shifting the miracle. When a miracle doesn't happen, believers will often claim another miracle happened instead, one less obviously miraculous. For example, imagine a child who has a heart condition. Everyone empathizes and prays for healing, but the healing does not materialize. But then the child turns out to be a very sweet person who makes everyone around them feel good; the kind of person who brightens the room they are in. At the funeral, believers now realize why God didn't heal her heart condition. It was because God wanted to perform a greater miracle: the miracle of showing his grace through her. And this could only have happened, it is affirmed, by giving this child a heart condition. This sort of move happens all the time among evangelical Christians, and it demonstrates that the engine driving belief in miracles is nothing more than the belief in miracles itself. No actual miracles are required! Once a person believes that miracles happen, they will happen everywhere and no number of facts about the real world will change this.

A cliche answer to the paucity of miraculous events and the lack of any consistent experience of the miraculous is that "God is not a vending machine." He is a person. He is not there just to perform tricks for you. God's supernatural interventions, Christians argue, are tied to his divine purposes for your life, not to the agenda of an atheist or a scientist. When in the gospels the Pharisees asked Jesus for a sign to prove his authority, he rebuffed them and refused, saying: "A wicked and adulterous generation looks for a miraculous sign" (Matthew 16:4). The suggestion is seemingly that there is enough evidence to be found already for those who are willing to look, so requests for more explicit proof show that ulterior motives are at work. Another related idea is that we should not test God. This is what the devil did when he suggested that Jesus prove his identity by throwing himself off the top of the temple, since God would not allow his son to die in such a manner. Jesus' answer, "Do not put the Lord your God to the test" (Matthew 4:7) is seen as a prohibition against any approach to God's miraculous activity that would attempt to measure or prove it. Are these real spiritual principles or are they just facile obfuscators that both the Bible and Christians have developed to cope with the fact that the supernatural world is just not reliable or verifiable? It seems to me that we should be suspicious any time a request for verification is treated as impertinent or inappropriate.

Any apologist worth his salt will have a ready answer for all the factors I've just listed. "Rob," they will aver, "nothing you have said here proves that miracles are impossible. Everything you said is actually true to one extent or another. I agree with you! But showing that many miraculous claims are sketchy does not disprove divine miraculous power."

And it's true. I can't disprove miracles categorically. I don't even want to. I would love to experience a miracle. Who wouldn't? But after about a half century of living a "supernatural" life, I have to admit: On the one hand I haven't seen anything even remotely like a miracle. On the other hand, I've seen patterned credulity on display over and over again, and so I know firsthand this ocean of credulity is vast. The question I'm asking is this: If the miracle claims people make can be explained by well-known deficiencies of the mind, then why do we have to bring a divine agent into it?

Imagine a time traveler from eight hundred years ago who is taken on an airplane. This person might be concerned because in their world people only fly by the power of demons. At least, this is what they believe. And so they are fearful and suspicious of the whole thing. But since it's a long trip, let's say that a modern guide explains the basic principles of flight, and our time traveler says he understands. The modern guide feels good about this and prepares to relax and enjoy the rest of the flight, as counselled by the stewardess. Suddenly though, the time traveler blurts out, "But I still think it might be the work of the devil." Why would he say this? He already knows the principles of flight and through them he already has a full explanation for the phenomenon he is experiencing. There is no need to appeal to a supernatural cause, or even to consider that a supernatural agent might somehow also explain the ability to make a plane fly. As the famous theologian and philosopher William of Occam would have insisted, "entities should not be multiplied beyond necessity." Once you have a full explanation, that's enough. Don't keep making things up after that point. Similarly, if luck, coincidence, credulity, psychology, and sociology can provide a full explanation for so-called miraculous phenomena, why put forward God or the supernatural as an explanation? The reason is that we humans have trouble letting go of strongly held ideas, even when the evidence is clearly against them. And so we multiply entities.

Maybe someday I will experience a true, incontrovertible miracle. If that happens, I will be very excited and I will happily acknowledge it and I probably won't shut up about it. But for the time being, I'm chalking the miraculous up to the foibles of human nature. And if anyone thinks I'm just hopelessly wrong about this, I invite them to perform a miracle in my presence.

CHAPTER 10
NO FIRM FOUNDATION

As we have seen, the faith of many, if not most, evangelical Christians is based on an accounting of how God has supposedly worked in their lives. But typically, the rationales for determining that God has been at work, that God has spoken to them, or that God has been watching out for them, are not compelling. There are many other explanations for the experiences these people have.

Let's take an example, based on an actual occurrence. A single mother loses her son to a freak kayaking accident. She panics and she questions her faith. The fact that she questions her faith shows that her faith is directly related to God's plan for her life. That is the core of the thing. Otherwise, this turn of events would not have affected her faith. After a year or two "in the wilderness," she has an experience and she interprets this as God touching her, or revealing his grace to her. She now becomes more open again to her faith. She is able now to affirm that God had a plan for her even in this extreme situation of loss, even if she does not understand it. But she can accept his "sovereignty." And then it becomes an emotionally powerful testimony. Everyone cries.

But isn't it fair to ask whether this is not just a natural

psychological (human) response to tragedy, mirroring the well-known and well-documented five stages of grief? Haven't evangelicals who see God's hand at work in this woman's life merely imbued a normal psychological process with spiritual significance? Haven't they inserted a divine agent into nature, and then "baptized" a natural process to treat it as though it were supernatural? And is there any compelling reason to affirm that God was involved in this at all? Many people go through tragedies and then recover, without bringing God into it. Therefore, the mere act of recovery is not itself evidence of anything supernatural at work. The sad tragedy is that many people have to give up God in their worst moments because nothing makes sense. When things get back to normal, however, they forget the incoherence and they come back and reaffirm the set of beliefs that abandoned them at their worst moment. This is because we live most of our lives in normal, stable circumstances. We aren't that good at handling the upheavals—that is the entire problem of upheavals. And yet, it is the upheavals which can, if we let them, reveal the incoherence of our beliefs.

THE POINTED QUESTION

What basis does anyone have for saying that something, be it a circumstance, an event, or a feeling, is from God? That it is not merely human. Not natural. That it has no physical explanation. What evidence is there that one thing or another definitely requires divine intervention for an explanation? This is the key question that lies at the center of Christianity's claims of truth—or any religious claim for that matter. Why should I believe any supernatural claim at all? Especially when the vast majority of supernatural claims are easily dismissed as the result of coincidence, luck, or the foibles of the mind.

We live our lives surrounded by natural phenomena that can be touched, seen, tested, investigated, and repeated over and over again with the same results. There is a consistency to the natural world, and that consistency allows us to plan our lives and exert at least some measure of control over our future. Plants bear fruit in the summer, so we can plan to get our food from them. Gasoline combusts under certain conditions, so we can harness that energy to travel and get things done. The sun rises and sets in a 24-hour cycle, so we can plan our days accordingly. Our lives are cyclical. We consume energy, be it by using a lightbulb or by expending biochemical energy when we walk, work, or study. We must replenish that energy. We engage in activities and then we rest. We go out, and we come back in. We lay down and we rise. We gather and talk, and then scatter and become silent. All of these patterns of behavior are possible because the world is also consistently patterned. The ultimate source of this patterned existence is astronomical: the earth has rotated on its axis and around the sun with such consistency and for so long that this has formed an environment in which we can thrive. And then, we also emerged from that same environment. The more we study our own patterns and the principles that govern them, the more we explain the world and the more control we gain over it. And the more we do this, the more we see that we have no need for the supernatural hypothesis. That is why the key question that needs to be put to any supernatural claim is, "What is it about this event that places it outside the cyclical and patterned world of physical phenomena?" But once the question is asked this explicitly, it becomes extremely difficult to answer. How could we determine that an event was caused by a supernatural agent? It would have to be something truly exceptional, public, repeatable, and palpable. But as we have seen in the previous chapter, claims of the miraculous never rise to this challenge. Rather, miraculous claims are invariably bolstered by misunderstanding, misconstruing, and wishful thinking, and they can easily shown to be so.

But there is something else too. The patterns of life are not entirely consistent. The sun may reasonably be relied on to rise every morning, but whether that day is cloudy, rainy, or clear is not as easy to predict. The seasons also reliably cycle through, but there is a great deal of variety within each cycle. Some winters are mild, others are extremely cold. Some summers lead to a full harvest, while others result in famine. Our gas-powered vehicle works most of the time, but it occasionally breaks down. Our bodies function very well on most days, but they can also be subject to the vicissitudes of variation and they can break down. It is precisely in these places where the cyclical reliability of the physical world breaks down that we are tempted to insert a nonphysical force or agent. This is because lack of reliability and predictability is dangerous and concerning. We made a plan to survive, to live, to thrive. But the weather, or our health, or circumstances conspired against us. And so, the idea of the supernatural arises in order to explain inconsistencies in the operation of the physical world. The affirmation of the supernatural is, ironically, an attempt to rationalize the world of experience. We find that it is better for our own peace of mind to generate explanations where none exist than to live with the idea that some things are just random and uncontrollable. We invent the supernatural in order to make sense of the natural. I say this is ironic, because belief in the supernatural is typically criticized for being irrational. But it is actually an attempt to achieve a higher level of rationality. We humans are always trying to make sense of the world, and if making sense of the world on a higher level of rationality means asserting minor irrationalities along the way, we happily indulge. It's no coincidence that the vast majority of miracle claims are connected to those areas of experience that break down most often, and which most notably threaten our ability to control our lives. Healing is at the top of the list, along with financial rescues, and then circumstantial salvations. But I don't see a lot of hoopla around the miracle of, say, levitation. Not being able to float in the air does not threaten our existence. It does not fill any gap of reliability that exists in the solidly predictable cycles of nature that define our lives. Miracles aren't about seeing something cool and amazing. They are about asserting, or seeming to assert, control over things which are unpredictable.

An example of the most superficial miracle claim, one which even some evangelicals mock, is that God made sure I got a parking place. We've all been there: We made plans, be it for an appointment, an important business meeting, or to meet an old friend. But there's nowhere to park! Control of the situation is slipping away moment by moment. All our plans suddenly seem to be hanging in the balance of what was supposed to be a very simple issue. We drive up and down the aisles of cars, scanning intently for an opening, keenly aware of competitors who are also on the prowl. Then, suddenly, there's an empty space! We quickly claim it with the feeling that we are special because things are going our way. Take a deep breath. The tension recedes. Control has been regained. And if we have already accepted the notion that there is something or someone greater, we give them credit for what appears to be a small miracle. But of course, in a crowded parking lot, people are experiencing this kind of thing all day long. Every time a parking space becomes available, as is bound to happen on a regular basis, whoever happens to come upon it is bound to be relieved when they have found an empty space. Conversely, many people do not find any parking and must make alternate arrangements. What is really happening here is that we are each taking turns at being the lucky person who happens to find a space in a full parking lot.

Of course, parking space miracles are not seriously presented as proof of the supernatural. (Or are they?) These are maintenance miracles that keep alive the faith of those who have already decided God is managing both the micro and macro dimensions of their lives. But parking lot miracles do provide a template for all other miracle claims, and perhaps, because of their simplistic absurdity, highlight the crucial problem of the miraculous: Just because something seems to be finely crafted for our benefit doesn't mean it is. In order for any supernatural claim to be taken seriously, it needs to be shown that it could not have been caused by the natural functioning of the world. And it is an unfortunate fact of the world that this is extremely difficult to do. For a miracle to be miraculous, we must first dispense with the more likely nonmiraculous options. In spite of this, believers regularly and casually attribute natural phenomena to God.

If Christianity is truly a supernatural religion, it ought to provide people with explicitly supernatural experiences. This idea came to my attention many years ago after reading a passage in 1 Corinthians:

> If an unbeliever or someone who does not understand comes in [to a church gathering] while everybody is prophesying, he will be convinced by all that he is a sinner and will be judged by all, and the secrets of his heart will be laid bare. So he will fall down and worship God, exclaiming, "God is really among you!" (1 Corinthians 14:24-25).

The Apostle Paul really seems to think that if someone walks into a room and is immediately told by a group of complete strangers that they are a horrible person, that person will have a positive reaction. That doesn't seem like the most likely scenario to me. Be that as it may, notice the important claim that church ought to be a place where God's supernatural work is compellingly on display, and that as a result of that supernatural activity—in this case the ability to divine a stranger's deepest secrets—people will be so amazed that they will break into spontaneous worship.

For a season, this passage became a guiding light for me. I loved the idea that the most convincing thing about Christianity was not a message, a sermon, or an appeal, but spiritual power on display for all to see. And I pursued that as an ideal. Unfortunately, it turned out that this was just another illusion. Another aspirational claim that Christianity cannot make good on. Let's compare the miraculous expectation of the passage above to reality. Some charismatic or Pentecostal preachers habitually claim from the pulpit that they have received a word from God about someone who is sitting in the congregation. "Someone here is struggling with... [fill in the blank]." It's usually some general ailment like discouragement, a troubled marriage, disappointment, or financial trouble. If the folks who make fortune cookies can come up with "fortunes" that seem to apply personally to everyone, then it's hardly compelling to see a preacher do it. Any group is bound to have people struggling with things like discouragement, loss of a job, a sick loved one, or a chronic inability to find parking spaces. The funny part is when a preacher makes a specific appeal—"Someone here is struggling with cancer"—and then multiple people respond, showing with complete clarity the name of the game. The preacher doesn't skip a beat, and the audience is even more amazed! And if no one answers, that's easy: just pretend they are shy and pray for them anyway. This is not a great fit for the expectation of the passage that people in the service will have "the secrets of [their] hearts laid bare" such that there is no other option than to fall down and worship God. This is just tawdry manipulation. It's not even clever or difficult to do.

I suppose the reason I was interested in this passage and the idea of a compelling demonstration of God's presence in the church service was a question that was slowly forming in my mind: Is there anything divine happening here at all, in these weekly gatherings, or is this just a group of people who come together for a common cause that happens to be religious? Is there any evidence that any of this churchly activity has a godly, supernatural source and is not explainable by the materialistic reality of human minds interacting in human groups? The answer, I now see, is no. There is no evidence of the supernatural in churches. There is hope, there is emotion, there is wishful thinking, and there is credulity. But nothing here is compellingly supernatural.

Time and time again, Christians assert highly subjective interpretations of things that happen to every human being as though they were evidence of God's love and activity in their lives, of God's loving management of their life story.

"I got a new job that I really wanted! Thank you, Lord!" But many people who don't have faith in God also get new jobs that they really wanted.

"My husband and I were going through a rough spot in our marriage, but the Lord helped us to appreciate each other more. Now we are doing really great." But many people who don't serve the Lord go through rough patches in their marriages and come out stronger than before.

"I was abused as a child, but when I read the Bible and started praying, God healed me and helped me forgive my abuser." But many abused people who don't pray, read the Bible, or appeal to God have also found healing and forgiven their abusers.

"We weren't sure if I should take the new job and move back to the city, but we prayed about it and the Lord gave us peace about the decision, so here we are." But many people are faced with difficult decisions and yet, without prayer, they achieve a sense that they made the right choice.

To be clear, I am not denying the power of religion to bring about personal transformation or give people meaning through the ups and downs of life. I'm only saying that the power of religion is mirrored in the lives of people who do not have religion. Because of this, the Christian conclusion that God is involved is not compellingly supported by the events. It is definitely not the case of something that can only be explained by the actions of God.

BELIEVE IN ORDER TO UNDERSTAND

The choice to interpret God as active in one's life is nothing more than that: an interpretive *choice* based on a foundational set of ideas. God loves me, God has a plan for my life, God is leading me, my life has meaning to God, Jesus died for my sins. The Christian interprets their experience in a way that is informed by these foundational ideas. But their experience does not prove the ideas. Therefore, the foundational ideas themselves are not verified or verifiable. They are mere assertions, mere ideas, mere claims which make sense because they make sense. People accept them because they have accepted them, not because there is any compelling evidence to accept them. There is no solid starting point, only a circular movement from the acceptance of unprovable ideas to the reinforcement of those ideas by experiences that don't prove them.

One of my former pastors was fond of saying something like this: "We could look at all the evidence for the existence of God and the truth of Christianity—and there is very good evidence—but today we are going to talk about what happens after we accept that God exists and loves us." Needless to say, he never got around to talking about "all the evidence." This is because evidence is beside the point in a Sunday sermon or in any other religious setting. No one really cares that much about evidence when it comes to religious convictions. It's nice to have it, but that's just not how the brain on religion handles information. First it accepts, then it sees evidence in the light of that acceptance.

I am by no means the first person to describe this sort of thinking. The idea that faith comes first, followed by understanding, is deeply Christian and was famously expressed by the medieval theologian Anselm of Canterbury. This is so important that in scholarly theological Christian circles it is often referred to in the original Latin: *credo ut intelligam*. I believe in order to understand. The first time I heard that expression, as a Christian, it made me uncomfortable. Speaking personally, I would rather understand first and then believe. Or at least be engaged in some sort of a dialog between belief and understanding. And this has always been the case for me, even when I was firmly entrenched in the evangelical Christian worldview. But that's just me. It doesn't seem to be the way this works for many. The vast majority of Christians believe first; then they understand. Or more to my point, belief comes first, *reasons for the validity of that belief* second.

HOW TO PROVE THE UNPROVABLE

This is the essence of Christian belief: A foundational set of ideas is accepted "by faith" as true. Then, after a person accepts the foundational ideas, they make an attempt to ground those ideas in experience, to show them at work. And this grounding is considered evidence. However, the evidence is not hugely compelling for those who are not already committed to the foundational ideas. It is only compelling to those who have accepted them.

While I'm picking on evangelical Christian religious faith here, this sort of deductive reasoning can be found everywhere in life. It may be more pronounced in religious thinking, but sloppy deductive reasoning is what the human brain does. Let's use something random and completely fabricated for an illustration. For example, let's put forward the idea that people are happier when their government makes all the important decisions in life for them: the choice of career, marriage, and where to live. Since the government is more objective, the argument might go, it can make better decisions than the individuals themselves, who view their lives too emotionally. Also, if the government can manage everyone such that society as a whole thrives, this will add to the happiness of individuals. I don't really believe this idea. I'm just using it as an example because it's the type of big picture belief that easily forms in people's minds, can conceivably motivate a political or social movement, and is also very difficult to verify one way or another.

Now, let's say that I'm already convinced of this big idea. I don't even have a clear notion of where I got it, but I like it and I like the picture of the world that it forms in my mind. In order to convince others, and also to reassure myself that I am right, I will go out into the world and try to find evidence for my big idea. For example, I might find people who have grown up in highly managed situations and are happy. I might also look for a society that prizes personal freedom and point to instances of tragedy and unhappiness in that society which stem from this freedom. None of this would be difficult to do, and it would seem compelling to those who already believe the big idea of a more managed society. However, this data, even though accurate, would not really prove as much as it might seem. The question is not whether some people are happy in managed situations, but whether all or most people would be happy in that situation. Besides, a limited sample might highlight people who are happy in a managed situation, but for reasons other than the managed situation. And the question is not whether some people who prize freedom are miserable because of it, but whether all or most people who exercise freedom are miserable. Further, would these miserable people be happier under the managed situation, or is their unhappiness something like mental illness that could always come to the surface in any political system?

The striking thing about the evidence in this example is that it seems compelling and is accurate, but it doesn't in fact prove anything at all because it is a limited sample, selected with an end goal in mind. The idea that compelling and true evidence does not necessarily prove something is unintuitive, but it is crucial. This subtle distinction is regularly trampled when big ideas are at stake.

Another name for this way of handling information is "confirmation bias," when we look only for a narrow set of data that confirms our view. We don't bother too much with other data that does not fit. The contrary data can be dismissed, explained away, or attributed to the machinations of bad people who don't like the goodness of our big idea. I think of this as *deductive* reasoning because the evidence is orchestrated by the big idea that has already been accepted and is already prized. The evidence is essentially deduced from the big idea. Because what the believer knows above all else is that the big idea must be true. But the big idea is not itself deduced from anything. It is merely accepted, merely stated, merely affirmed.

CHAMPIONS OF SUBJECTIVITY

A better approach to verifying the accuracy or desirability of a big idea would be to start without a big idea at all. In the case of my hypothetical political idea that says people are happier when they are managed by the government, we could start with an open-ended question: What type of government makes people happy? Then we could go about building an answer based on what we discover. This is usually thought of as *inductive* thinking. Starting from the data and building a model that takes all of it into account. It is roughly what science and reason try to do, even if they are not always successful, due to the myriad challenges presented by human nature. The inductive approach doesn't mean starting without any preexisting ideas. That is clearly difficult to do when it comes to big and controversial questions like whether we can see evidence of God's love and direction of our lives, or what type of political arrangement makes people happy. Most people probably already have some kind of an answer to these questions before they are even aware of them. The issue is not whether we have previously conceived answers. The issue is how we treat those. If our preconceived answers are provisional, open to change, open to being falsified, then that is OK. This does not get in the way of a more objective approach to the evidence. But if it is already a given that our ideas are fixed and cannot be challenged, it will be difficult to remain open to the evidence.

However, evangelical religious thinking wreaks havoc on objectivity and the intellectual flexibility needed to investigate the world through inductive reasoning. In fact, Christian religious thinking represents one of the most serious challenges to inductive reasoning.

Evangelical thinking starts with fixed ideas rather than with exploration, and these fixed ideas cannot be questioned. The ideas are quite ancient and are not always compatible with advances in knowledge that have occurred since they originated. But commitment to them is absolutely required in order to participate. They are not open to debate, and they are not to be questioned in the light of other observed phenomena.

Evangelicals inhabit social structures which ensure these fixed ideas are deeply internalized and not questioned. Religion is often a family affair, and the religious family functions as a pressure mechanism to keep members of the family in line. This principle can be extended to social networks outside of the family. Religious adherence generates friendship and even business relations which are ultimately dependent on a shared orthodoxy. I'm not suggesting some religious person sat down and thought up all these things to keep people in line. This is just how people work and how social dynamics are bound to develop. People who share a common view of the world will, like birds of a feather, flock together. And being part of the flock generates incredible pressure to think about the world in a certain way. I used to regularly observe a striking example of how this works. When I happened to be teaching on some topic or another, a participant would raise their hand and ask, "But what do *we* believe about this?" It always irked me, and I sometimes gave in to my irritation and responded with, "Well, I don't know what *you* believe, but I'm happy to explain what *I* believe about it." But of course, once I explained my own thoughts, they were bound to be extremely influential in the mind of the person who asked the question. I was still then under the mistaken impression that religion and independent thinking could go together.

The very notion of accepting ideas noncritically is heroized in evangelical religious thinking and turned into a virtue. It gets its own name—"faith." And faith is then imbued with a moral value. It is good to have faith, and it is bad to not have it.

The coup-d'état of evangelical religious thinking against objectivity is that behind all these more benign distorting pressures there is also the threat of eternal hell for noncompliance. The threat of hell applies not only to believers, but in fact to everyone on the planet. If you fail to accept these fixed ideas, which cannot be subjected to critical thinking and which are not open to discussion, an eternity of excruciating pain awaits you.

All of this, again, adds up to the worst possible scenario for thinking objectively: pushing fixed ideas (orthodoxies), praising subjectivity, and using threats of torture for those who don't accept the fixed ideas. Is it any wonder that believers are constantly at odds with the discoveries of science and the conclusions of reason? And again, I have to ask, who commends subjectivity and relies on threats of torture to maintain ideological purity? Probably those who don't have evidence on their side. Because, after all, wouldn't evidence be a much easier sell? And in our current more sensitive and compassionate climate, wouldn't anyone who has evidence favor using it as opposed to the highly controversial move of bringing out eternal damnation? I've always thought that resorting to nonevidence is a sure admission of defeat. Because everyone prizes evidence. And if you got it, you use it. Only people who don't have confidence in the evidence appeal to subjectivity and threats. Similar to the mother who tells her kids that if they keep misbehaving the police will come and take them away. She only deploys this threat because she's at her wit's end and doesn't know what else to do. The threat of violence is the last resort of those who hold an untenable idea.

CHAPTER 11
UNMASKING CONVERSION

HOW TO GET SAVED

The alignment of the mind to a big idea is not random. What motivates people to embrace a big idea, and a religious one in particular, in the first place?

People often come to belief as the result of a religious experience. They encounter something they can't explain, they have an insight that seems too sublime for normal explanations, or they have an intense emotional experience that is so unique that they label it as "spiritual."

Because it's the way they grew up. This is probably the most common reason people are intuitively drawn to a big idea. It is what they were taught as children and this left a mark. The mind has difficulty tracking the difference between what is true and what is familiar, and things that are familiar tend to seem true. That is why, counter to our intuition, mere repetition does actually change people's minds. Many Americans grow up going to church, but then go their own way when they get out on their own, only to return to church later in their adult life—sometimes because they now have kids of their own and want to replicate their own upbringing. In fact, I suspect that the majority of adult converts to Christianity were exposed to it as children. I've heard that testimony many times.

Because the idea is expressed by someone they admire, like a friend, a romantic partner, or a family member. We are far more susceptible to the ideas and attitudes of our peers than we realize. Clearly, people who spend time together tend to have similar opinions and beliefs. That's why ideas can often be tracked by regions or even by countries and why family members often share a common worldview. Friendships start because of commonalities, and they continue by establishing new shared experiences and commonalities. In evangelical circles there is an evangelistic strategy called "friendship evangelism." It was explicitly crafted from the well-researched fact that many people become Christians because of the influence of their friends.

Because of social proof. In the Billy Graham evangelistic crusades of previous generations, thousands of people would come together in a very large auditorium or stadium to hear a tall, good looking, white American talk about the important things in life. Then, at the end there was an invitation to come forward to "dedicate your life to Jesus" or to "get saved." Suddenly, people started pouring down the aisles and you might think, boy, everyone is really into this. Maybe there's something to it! And you go down with everyone and it becomes an emotional experience. Gathering with others to listen to the same voice, to sing together, to chant together, to have a common experience—these are all very powerful opinion-forming events. Mass gatherings are one striking example of social proof, but this can occur wherever an individual is exposed to many other people who affirm the validity of an idea or attitude.

People in vulnerable situations will tend to be open to new ideas and social networks, particularly if they are welcomed and accepted. Another well-known evangelism strategy is to start ministries targeting individuals who are new to an area or in transition. A popular target is international students at colleges and universities. They are eager to learn about their new culture and they find themselves without the regular social and intellectual structures that regulate their thinking and activity in their home countries. Because of this, international students are more open to a new message and a new religion. Most universities have a Christian ministry dedicated to reaching international students. Another approach is ministries to the homeless. While these do provide much needed material help, they typically include an evangelistic component, as when, for example, people who come to a local mission are forced to sit through a Christian service to partake of the food or stay for the night.

Because of a good story. It is human nature to love a good story. That is why stories have been a feature of human culture and thought as far back as we can see, and it is why sharing stories and the technology that surrounds them are one of the biggest businesses on the planet. Good stories capture the imagination and the emotions. This is especially true if the story seems to tell us something about ourselves. Stories are so compelling that if we are sufficiently engaged by them, we don't even think to ask whether they are true or not. The brain just skips this step and moves straight to acceptance. And religion always comes with a good story. In fact, there is no major religion without a good story: the story of a hero, of a quest for enlightenment, of the origin of all things, of the future, of the discovery of the self. If the story is compelling, people will believe it and "accept it into their lives." Evangelists are well aware of the power of story and this is why evangelical lay people are invariably taught to use their own testimony as the primary tool for their own evangelistic efforts. Telling a good story about how Jesus changed your life is much more persuasive than arguing about some abstract point of theology. A story builds trust and rapport. It makes big ideas relatable and believable.

But isn't there a category of reasons missing? What about

people who accept a big idea because they arrived at it through intellectual rigor? Like Diogenes, they went out into the world seeking for truth, and after studying all the data, considering the possibilities, and listening to all the arguments, they found the one true answer which explained all of human history, life, the universe, and everything. The reason this category is missing is that, well, it's missing. Very few people become a Christian or a Muslim or a Buddhist because of research. That sort of intellectual rigor is beyond the reach of most people. Even more accessible versions of this, like reading just a single book about the major world religions, are extremely rare. It's also difficult to find an unbiased account of all religions. They are all written by people with previous religious (or nonreligious) commitments. The idea that no one becomes a Christian as a result of an intellectual argument is well-known among those who think about evangelism and practice it. As an intellectual, I always found this discouraging. My natural tendency is to generate arguments based on facts. But as it turns out, facts are not very important when it comes to conversion. I have to admit that facts were not crucial in *my* becoming a Christian. I grew up that way. Once people accept a big idea, though, they become interested in supporting it, demonstrating it, and proving it, and that is why such herculean efforts go into trying to prove Christianity. This effort is posited as an outreach to unbelievers, but the faithful are also the target audience. They are perhaps the only real one.

For the most part, people accept big ideas because of the human dynamics surrounding the idea, not on the merit of the ideas themselves. While believers tend to attribute new conversions to the work of God and the conviction of the Holy Spirit, we are faced with the same problem I've already highlighted: Is there anything about these conversion events that points definitively to a supernatural agent? The answer is that none of it requires supernatural intervention. It is all well within the bounds of what is humanly possible, common, and even predictable.

Some people claim their conversion experience was uniquely powerful and must have been from God. But of course, intense or unique experiences don't prove a lot. For one thing, people in different religions all have intense religious experiences. While each adherent will maintain their type of experience is unique or true in comparison with religious experiences in other religions, this is extremely difficult to prove. When people have an experience in a particular religious-cultural context, they will tend to associate it with the religious options that are available to them, and so a "content neutral" feeling becomes attached to a particular big idea. Additionally, though it can be hard for religious people to understand this, nonreligious people also have intensely emotional experiences and insights. The most we can say about these sorts of experiences is that they seem to be a feature of the human mind. They may point to something spiritual, something "beyond," but this is difficult to demonstrate.

Welcome to human nature, to psychology, to the foibles of human decision-making and motivation. This has been understood, if incompletely, for millennia. Behavioral patterns can be discerned. We are all subject to them. But in the modern world we have begun to look at all these factors systematically, and the expanding body of knowledge is a growing question mark that hovers over the very concept of conversion. How much of what seems to be a supernatural work of God in the hearts of people who were "convicted by the Holy Spirit" can be accounted for by some basic principles that are well-documented by psychology? It turns out that the deeper we look, the more questions we ask, and the more comparisons we make to other areas of life, the more this all looks merely human. All the seemingly supernatural elements of conversion evaporate, and we are left with the workings of the human mind.

The psychology of conversion brings up the specter of

manipulation. It's no accident that modern corporations have embraced the term "product evangelism" to describe their promotional efforts. To what extent do preachers and leaders know these psychological principles and use them? For example, in the Billy Graham crusades there was a bit of a trick to swelling the number of people who came down the aisle. The invitation was not just to accept Jesus as a new believer, but there was also an appeal to believers to "rededicate" their lives. So while it might seem like dozens of non-Christians are now choosing to become Christians at the altar call, the stream of supplicants making their way down the isles is a mix of new converts and existing believers. You have to prime the pump somehow. Very few individuals would walk down the aisle in front of fifty thousand other people if it was just them. Some Christian traditions have rejected the whole idea of asking people to "walk down the aisle" or "do an altar call" precisely because it is too problematic and manipulative. And the idea that we should make friends with people in order to evangelize them is clearly fraught with difficulties. It seems insincere and manipulative. It is similar to becoming someone's friend so that you can sell them something. Religious multilevel marketing. Reaching out to people in vulnerable situations with ulterior motives seems predatory, to say the least.

But that's not to say that seemingly manipulative practices are always cynically deployed. Sometimes they are just traditions: They are done because they have always worked. The effectiveness of a psychological trick can be masked by the conviction that the Holy Spirit is the one doing the converting. Sometimes people just notice what works and they do it, without thinking about the implications or being consciously manipulative. Many evangelical Christians are also capable of mining questionable conversion techniques without any sense that they are being manipulative. This is because they have already accepted the big religious idea that everyone needs conversion. So what if people become Christians as a result of arguably manipulative practices? If you think that your big idea is the most important thing in the world, then any means of persuasion might seem justified.

The effect of all these techniques and factors that I've described is that conversion is unmasked. The idea that there is a supernatural agent behind conversion, a revelation, or "being born again" becomes less and less credible when we consider all the non-supernatural patterns and motivations that we know are at work.

Because, after all, we can look at a political movement—such as the way that Hitler motivated his followers in the 1930s—and find the same marks: powerful emotional gatherings, social proof, the assertion of ideas that have always seemed to be true, the influence of parents, friends, and acquaintances, and compelling proofs that appeal to confirmation bias. I'm not suggesting that religious people are like Nazis. Of course not. The point is that a powerful political movement looks a lot like a religion and the two gather and maintain adherents in similar ways. But people don't generally attribute a political movement to God. This all lands us back at the important point I've been chasing: *it is unrealistic to attribute everything we see at work in religion to God if psychology accounts for it.*

WHAT I LEARNED FROM MORMON MISSIONARIES

The idea that people can be converted by manufactured religious experiences came home to me very clearly when I invited some Mormon missionaries to come into my home. If you have not had a visit from a couple of young men dressed in suits with the incongruous title of "elder," you are among the few. Perhaps the blessed few. In Mormonism, which is a variation of Christianity, young people are encouraged to dedicate two years of their life to mission work, which for the young men sometimes involves going door to door to win people over to their faith.

One time when they came knocking, I decided to hear them out. After our initial conversation, we agreed to meet again. I also invited some of my fellow evangelicals over, and our gathering became a bit of an experiment. Over a period of several weeks the young Mormon elders explained to us, with a great deal of conviction and passion, an absurd story involving a nineteenth-century preacher named Joseph Smith, angels, and nonexistent pre-Columbian cultures. According to the Book of Mormon, ancient Jews traveled across the Indian and Pacific Oceans to Central or South America (the exact location is not clear) and developed a flowering civilization for which no archeological evidence exists. Later, in about the fourth century, it was all destroyed, and the cursed survivors became the ancestors of Native Americans.

The story is absurd and racist, and I have never wavered in my unbelief of that tale. It was clearly concocted in the early nineteenth century when many outlandish theories about the origins of Native Americans were in circulation, and when very little was known on a popular level about pre-Columbian history in Central and South America. Even today, what happened two thousand years ago in those regions is not clear to many people. The challenge to me came in a different form. When I expressed my rational difficulties with the Mormon account, the elders did not even try to answer them with historical evidence. That was the argument I was ready for. But when I asked my questions about evidence, they seemed a bit puzzled and then, after considering for a few moments, made vague references to archeological finds, and said they knew an elder who had studied this. Would I like him to come sometime to answer my questions? But they clearly didn't think the problems I was raising were very important, referring to them as mere "material" questions. They wanted to talk about spiritual questions. That is what they were trained for and that is what they wanted to focus on.

Instead of engaging with the historical evidence surrounding the story of the Book of Mormon, the missionaries told me I should pray, and that God would give me a feeling which would confirm its veracity. Mormons are very specific about this feeling of conviction, which they often refer to as a "burning in the bosom." Basically, it's a sense of excitement in the chest that is interpreted as a confirming sign from God. This is religious thinking at work. If the evidence doesn't line up, change the topic to something more subjective. I could have argued with this and pointed out that no amount of prayer was going to change the fact that the story of the Book of Mormon was highly unlikely in the light of what is known about pre-Columbian America. But I played along and prayed the prayer, on my own time. When I reported at the next meeting that no feeling of conviction had overcome me, I was told that I should pray more. To this I responded, "I have no motivation to pursue a feeling for something that I already know is not true." The Mormon religious experience is not reliably transferable from person to person. Just because the Mormon missionaries had experienced a burning in the bosom, it didn't mean I would. But clearly, the burning in the bosom does sometimes work because people are suggestible and gullible. If you tell them to have a subjective experience, especially a very mild and vague one, they will often go off and have it, and proceed to give it more weight in their thinking than it deserves. Mormon missionaries are also setting up a kind of psychological experiment that is optimized to produce feelings of nervousness or subtle excitement (the two feelings can be hard to distinguish): A person who prays for an experience will tend to do so with a sense of expectation, especially if the prayer has already been embedded in the question of converting to a new religion. "I'm not sure if this is true or not. But could it be? What if I do have a feeling? Does this mean I have to join their church? What will that be like? Could it mean I discovered the ultimate meaning of life?" All these thoughts, or something like them, will be swirling around in the mind of the person making the prayer. I know because even I, a self-confident rationalist, was unaccountably dealing with them when I prayed the prayer. This means that the request itself produces a certain amount of nervousness which can feel a lot like a "burning in the bosom." Is this a clever psychological trick that was cynically engineered for proselytizing? I suspect not. I say this because Mormons themselves rely on these kinds of feelings to make decisions. More likely, it is just a habit that developed through practice. It's just something that works and is perpetuated by the fact that it continues to work. Even the practitioners themselves fall for their own trick.

Throughout the meetings with the Mormon elders, I was struck by the powerful conviction of these young missionaries. They really thought they had the truth, and they were visibly distressed at my lack of faith. And yet they were wrong. Of course, passionate error is nothing new. But here is what really troubled me: Most evangelical Christians I knew had come to faith or maintained their belief by the same types of arguments that the Mormons were using, where subjective experiences were used to confirm unprovable beliefs. Prayer, notable circumstances, and emotional phenomena were granted much greater authority than rational considerations. There was not, in Mormonism or in evangelical Christianity, a search for verifiable information. On the contrary, information was consistently subsumed to emotion and authority. Christianity does have a massive credibility advantage over Mormonism. At least the Bible talks about places that really existed. There really is historical validation for a great deal of the information that is found in the Christian scriptures. But still, the subjective religious mechanisms that bring about belief are the same in Mormonism and in evangelical Christianity. If you doubt, pray. If you question, meet with an elder or read a book that tells you otherwise. If you experience something troubling, have the faith to push through. Look inside, listen to the still small voice of God. But don't seek objective evidence. That's not helpful.

At the time I was troubled. How could I explain this concurrence between the methods of Mormonism and my own evangelical Christianity? The implication was hard to shake: If I think Mormons can be wrong, and they use the same types of arguments I use, then it is also possible that I may be wrong. Or, put another way: I had observed with complete clarity how a religious group could manufacture a "spiritual" result. Then it had dawned on me that my own religious group did the exact same thing. I didn't immediately onboard all the implications of this. Rather, this experience became an important insight that over time opened the possibility of other ideas.

It is profoundly hypocritical for evangelical Christians to criticize Mormons because of their subjectivity when evangelicals do the exact same thing. This hypocrisy goes unnoticed because of the different sets of beliefs. But the method is the same: Seek an experience. Then allow that experience to guide your understanding. Skip all the hard questions.

HAVING YOUR CAKE AND EATING IT TOO

I've always been confused about something regarding faith. On the one hand, we are supposed to believe in things which cannot be seen, things that do not have sufficient evidence. That's clear enough. But on the other, evangelical Christians are constantly talking about evidence too. It's called apologetics. Under this rubric one can learn all about arguments for the existence of God, how the Bible made amazing predictions that could only have come from a divine source, how to make sense of the existence of evil, why miracles are true, and more. And I want to ask, which one is it? Am I supposed to believe without evidence, or am I supposed to believe *because of* the evidence? I'm all in on the second one—at least as a method. Let's talk about the evidence and let's believe what the evidence supports. But then, where does faith come in?

The appeal to evidence implies reasoning from demonstrable facts, but this is incompatible with the imperative to rely on faith. Faith is a response to revelation from God. And revelations from God are supernatural and cannot be proven by evidence. They are, like the Big Bang, singularities beyond which it is impossible to look because the normal rules of evidence don't apply. How can reason prove a revelation? It never can. Revelation breaks the rules of evidence, by definition, because it tells us things that reason never could. And so, apologetics must forever serve revelation, it must forever accept first, believe first, and then reason based on the belief, even if it often pretends to do otherwise.

This points back to what I've already described, namely, that in evangelical thinking, and possibly in all religious thinking, the acceptance of certain crucial and nonnegotiable ideas comes first. Then, after that acceptance comes the search for evidence that supports it. But that evidence always gets the short end of the stick. Evidence is great when it affirms the things that are accepted by faith. But there isn't a lot of interest in evangelical circles in evidence itself, or in thinking clearly about evidence. And when the evidence falls short, the believer goes back to where it all started: not evidence, but belief. So, it's really a matter of wanting to have your cake and eat it too. There's a built-in permission to be sloppy. "We like evidence!" says the evangelical, "so long as it proves our point. But when the evidence brings up difficult questions, we reserve the right to toss it out and appeal to faith." This is the same pattern we encountered when discussing "God's plan for your life." Christians eagerly share stories about God's work in their lives with each other. Positive evidence is always welcome. But negative evidence, as when God doesn't provide, is handled by faith. It's a mystery. It will all make sense eventually. Just keep believing. Negative evidence doesn't get the same authority as positive evidence. It turns out that this deeply ingrained habit runs through evangelical Protestantism at all levels.

How can you even have a serious conversation with someone who thinks like this? It's like talking with your teenager:

> "I want to talk about last night," you say.
> "Oh, absolutely. I'm happy to talk about anything that happened last night," she answers.
> "So, you had your friends over and it sounded like you were having a lot of fun," you continue.
> "Yes, we had a wonderful time. Thank you for letting us hang out," beams your teenager.
> "I also see that your room is strewn with empty beer cans," you continue.
> To this, your teenager answers, "Oh, I have no idea where those came from!"

The teen is happy to talk about anything that happened—until difficult-to-explain evidence is presented. Now the strategy shifts: *mystery*! Evangelicals need to make up their minds. If they want to use evidence, then they should use it and stick to the rules of evidence. But if they are ultimately going to be guided by faith, then they should just go with that and stop wasting everyone's time.

CHAPTER 12
CONSCIENTIOUS OBJECTOR

JOURNEY INTO DARKNESS

I did not go out searching for unbelief. Rather, it caught up with me. I consciously resisted it. I had to use dreams and visions to reveal it to myself. I need to highlight this because there's always a personal judgment when people stop believing, as if the nonbeliever has done something wrong. For believers, unbelief must be the result of listening to the wrong voices or thinking the wrong thoughts, of not staying the course and fighting the good fight. Ultimately, they say, it is sourced in sin. It is bad. It is faithless. Once one has internalized this judgmental posture, it is extremely difficult to be objective about one's own lack of faith. Even the terms "unbelief" or "unbeliever" negatively bias the assessment of how and why one became an unbeliever. In fact, I am not really an unbeliever—I believe many things. It's just that I don't believe certain Christian ideas.

When it turns out your friend was untrustworthy, you remember other clues to his character that you should have noticed all along. In the same way, believers realize that those who no longer believe left clues behind, providing telling details about why they fell into this state of apostasy. The faithful pour over this evidence with dreadful fascination.

Those who care to pursue that sort of remembrance in my case could point to me being too intellectual, to me not ever really having a "vital" or "experiential" faith. And maybe there is something to that. Possibly, I was just never totally convinced. I don't know. But I feel like my faith was sincere! *If I myself don't know, then who does?* As I look back, it feels more like a dizzying swirl of possibilities spinning around in my head than a battle for belief. It was a garden of intellectual delights, and I didn't pay enough attention to the signs that said which trees I was supposed to eat from because those signs seemed artificial, disingenuous, or irrelevant. I had a good theological education and I'm thankful for it. I was taught to listen to contrary voices. I was castigated by my teachers for my unwarranted biases. I was taught to prize analysis and objectivity. But in the end, all these valuable intellectual tools pointed me in the wrong direction. Now the voices I remember best from my religious education are the secular ones, the ones I once critiqued. Their ideas were so compelling that they stuck with me, and the ones that called me to "believe first" have faded away.

The most memorable and influential class in my entire seminary education was a graduate seminar that introduced students to some of the important historical voices that had either rejected or significantly reinterpreted traditional Christianity. Every week we would read a classic, be it from David Hume, Immanuel Kant, Friedrich Hegel, Ludwig Feuerbach, or various other dead white guys. And every week, for three hours, we would discuss the book we had read. This was the inner sanctum of theology and philosophy. We were opening the hood of Christianity and experimenting with the engine. I sometimes drove home from these classes on an intellectual high. I might as well have been on drugs. It was exhilarating.

And it wasn't because I thought these authors and ideas were destroying my Christian faith and I found this somehow daring and exciting. It was because, on the one hand, I felt that some of their critiques missed the mark, and it was empowering to know that I had a seat at the table in this discussion and could hold my own. On the other hand, I thought some of their ideas deserved to be incorporated into the Christian worldview, and this opened up new and unforeseen possibilities. But it's interesting how the mind works and how good ideas have an effect over time. It's a bit like panning for gold, or sifting through the chaff to keep the wheat, only the process is much slower. But little by little the notions that best explain how the world really is and how it works are the ones that stay around and show their worth, while inept and fuzzy thinking dissipates.

The journey a conscientious person must take from belief to unbelief can be incredibly painful, lonely, emotionally draining, full of self-doubt and self-accusations—with entire dark days lost to depression—and it can place enormous strain on close personal relationships. I remember hearing a quote of Voltaire's many years ago, a voice which in retrospect feels like a powerful portent. I have to wonder why, out of all the things I've heard over the years, this one quote became so memorable. In a conversation about someone who had given up their faith in Christianity, Voltaire quipped, "He had to change his religion, and that always costs an honest man something."[1] It's true.

Those who are most exposed to the information that can bring about a change of mind are often the same people who make a living within the circle of belief: pastors, seminary and Bible school professors, leaders, popular authors, and speakers. For people who doubt in those situations, keeping their job becomes an added burden, a ball and chain that keeps them in the fold, at least pretending to believe or perhaps, as in my case, failing to admit to themselves their own disbelief. How can you, when your livelihood and your entire resume is connected to this set of beliefs? Having been one myself, I don't doubt that there are many evangelical Christian leaders who are just going through the motions, telling their flocks what they want to hear because they don't know how to do anything else, but if given the option to get out of ministry, they would gladly leave. Pursuing a career that depends on your ideological purity is a bad idea.

HOLY GHOST LIGHTING

One of the key theological problems that comes with evangelical thinking and traditional historic Christianity as a whole, is the ethics of belief. Christian doctrine states that if you believe wrongly, you are guilty of sin. Failure to believe is the original sin, in fact. In the garden of Eden, which witnessed the prototypical rebellion, Eve believed the serpent instead of God and she ate of the fruit that God had forbidden. And this one act of unbelief is said to have unleashed sinful nature and its horrific consequences on the world. In Christianity unbelief is, in a sense, the only sin. This is because the message of the Gospel is that you are saved, not by being a good person, but by believing in Jesus. This "saving faith" is what gets you into heaven. Therefore, unbelief is the only sin God can't set aside. It's the only sin that irrevocably cuts you off from his forgiveness.

The idea that salvation is tied to belief is unmissable in the Bible, the New Testament in particular.

- In the gospel of Mark, Jesus begins his ministry with the following proclamation, which is presented as a kind of summary of his entire message: "Jesus went into Galilee, proclaiming the good news of God. 'The time has come,' he said. 'The kingdom of God has

come near. Repent and *believe* the good news!'" (Mark 1:14-15).
- In the book of Romans, the Apostle Paul says, "if you confess with your mouth that Jesus is Lord, and believe in your heart that God raised him from the dead, you will be saved. For it is with your heart that you *believe* and are justified, and it is with your mouth that you confess and are saved." (Romans 10:9-10).
- Acts 16:31 has a clear, formulaic feel to it: "*Believe* in the Lord Jesus, and you will be saved—you and your household."
- And then there is the ubiquitous John 3:16, which can be seen on freeway signs and on posters at football games across the land, "For God so loved the world that he gave his one and only Son, that whoever *believes* in him shall not perish but have eternal life."

This much is clear, both in the Bible and in Christian teaching: to get saved, you gotta believe.

But there is a strange idea embedded in all this that seems to mostly go unnoticed. It's the implication that people have a choice in matters of belief. Is this realistic? Is this how the mind works? Can we really simply decide to believe something? My own path seems to suggest otherwise. As I mentioned previously, my brain seems to have decided what I believed without any input from my day-to-day conscious thinking. It seems the human mind integrates new information about the world automatically. When we perceive that something is true or real, we are intuitively convinced by the force of evidence or rationality. Belief is an automatic response to our understanding of the world. This is simply how the brain works. For confirmation, notice how our emotions change seemingly instantaneously when we are faced with new situations and information.

- Driving along the highway, you realize the car in front of you is sitting in the middle of the road. Suddenly, your heart is beating hard and you slam on the brakes. Your entire body has reacted to this new perception before you could even think about it.
- You are a child, and your parents sit you down to explain that they are splitting up. Your emotional response will be extreme and instant as your mind copes with all the implications of this world-shattering event.
- If you have a conversation with someone who challenges your most deeply cherished values and you don't know how to answer them, you will again find yourself in a state of emotional arousal, as though under attack. Because you are indeed under attack. Your perception of the world is under attack. Your mind has recognized this, and it has responded to this new perception by altering your emotional state.

Of course, not all beliefs form instantaneously. Some take years to develop. I'm only using the examples of emotional reactions to show that the process of belief formation has a mind of its own. It is not unlike breathing or the circulatory system. Belief formation is something the brain does whether we ask it to or not, as the brain seamlessly integrates new information, ideas, and the direct perceptions of the five senses into a coherent mental image of the world. Here's the crucial point: If our perceptions and previous understanding of the world form our beliefs in an automatic process, how can we go around asking people to change what they believe? How can we ask people to choose to believe something? And on what basis can we hold people blameworthy for their lack of belief?

But it is also true that we can interfere, to an extent, with the process of belief formation. We have many words to describe this, like denial, self-deception, willful ignorance, wishful thinking, and compartmentalization. Because there are times when our perception of the world is so painful it overwhelms us, and in those situations, we literally sabotage our belief formation faculties in order to maintain some semblance of stability. For some people, their belief-forming faculties are permanently damaged, and they cannot form a coherent mental image of the world. We call this mental illness, and it comes in many varieties. This raises an important question: When Christianity insists that we must believe certain things in order to receive God's forgiveness, or in order to enjoy life in heaven, or threatens us with eternal torture if we fail to believe certain things, isn't it forcing us to do something unnatural? Isn't it asking us to indulge in the sabotage of our mental faculties? Self-deception, denial, and the other methods we use to hide our true beliefs from ourselves are ultimately unhealthy and self-destructive. When people are caught up in these behaviors, they are not able to enjoy life to the fullest, their moral faculties can be impaired, their mental development stymied, and their view of themselves is distorted. This is not how belief formation is supposed to work. The brain has evolved such that information about the world should flow seamlessly to the mind and there form an accurate, or as accurate as possible, view of the world. And so it seems that Christianity, in its totalitarian demand that everyone must believe a specific set of ideas, is asking people to engage in a damaging psychological activity, and Christians would apparently be happy if everyone subverted their natural faculties in order to achieve the belief that God supposedly demands.

You can't demand belief from people. On the one hand, it tends to not work, because beliefs are etched on our brains as a result of factors which are often out of our control. On the other hand, there is the very real danger of badgering someone, or gaslighting them with sufficient pressure, into subverting their natural faculties to produce a confession of belief that amounts to psychological sabotage.

THE PURPORTED POWER OF THE GOSPEL

Descriptions in the Bible of people accepting the "good news" and getting saved also perpetuate this unrealistic view of how belief works. For example, throughout the gospels Jesus regularly meets random people, tells them to follow him, and they do so immediately and without hesitation. Life decisions are being made right there, in the moment. Why? Because, goes the subtext, these individuals are being confronted with something greater than themselves and responding appropriately. The preaching of the gospel is the narrative of *encounter*. Accept it or reject it. There will not be a Q&A session afterwards. Throughout the book of Acts, the part of the Bible that recounts the expansion of Christianity from Jerusalem to Rome, people similarly hear the message and are, so to speak, blown over by it and immediately believe. Sometimes they even start to speak in angelic tongues. This is not persuasion. It is conversion. Immediate, radical, complete. It is not even presented as having an intellectual component. In fact, the opposite is the case. Intellect gets in the way. The following passage is worth quoting at length because it shows the Apostle Paul's view of the task of preaching the gospel.

> For Christ did not send me to baptize, but to preach the gospel —not with wisdom and eloquence, lest the cross of Christ be emptied of its power. For the message of the cross is foolishness to those who are perishing, but to us who are being saved it is the power of God. For it is written:
> "I will destroy the wisdom of the wise; the intelligence of the intelligent I will frustrate."
> Where is the wise person? Where is the teacher of the law? Where is the philosopher of this age? Has not God made

foolish the wisdom of the world? For since in the wisdom of God the world through its wisdom did not know him, God was pleased through the foolishness of what was preached to save those who believe. Jews demand signs and Greeks look for wisdom, but we preach Christ crucified: a stumbling block to Jews and foolishness to Gentiles, but to those whom God has called, both Jews and Greeks, Christ the power of God and the wisdom of God (1 Corinthians 1:17-24).

For anyone interested in rationality, evidence, or wisdom, this passage says it all. "Move along. You can't accept this message by using your brain. You need foolishness to arrive at the believing state." In other words, the Bible seems to commend the subversion of our natural faculties, if this is what it takes to arrive at the believing state. But why are signs (evidence) and wisdom (rationality) so objectionable to Paul? Could it be for the utterly simple reason that the message of the gospel cannot be proven by evidence or deduced from rationality? The funny thing is that this is barely even controversial to Christians. Many would just say, "You're right. It can't be proven by evidence and reason. Amen!" But then, they demand that everyone believe it!

For Paul, the gospel is the power of God, and God has his privileged channels of communication. He doesn't use the regular rules of evidence and reason to convince you to believe. As Paul later explains, "The spiritual man makes judgments about all things, but he himself is not subject to any man's judgment" (1 Corinthians 2:15). It seems to me that if any contemporary religious charlatan came up with something like this, we would all just laugh out loud at them. "Oh really, you know everything because God told you? *Interesting…*" But since it's in a revered religious text, it gets away with sounding profound and mysterious.

Paul had his moment among the philosophers of the age, and it arguably didn't go well. Perhaps that experience is behind Paul's animosity here in 1 Corinthians. Acts 17 recounts that Paul visited Athens, the ancient center of philosophy, where he dialogued with, or perhaps preached at, stoics and epicurean philosophers, telling them that Jesus has been resurrected from the dead and they should all repent. A handful of people believed, but the overall reception was not amazing. If told today, the story would have taken place at Harvard or Oxford, and the result would have been the same: "I told them the truth, but they did not accept it because they refused to believe. They trusted in their logic, instead of the gospel." The passage is dripping with dismissiveness, as when the people at Athens are described thus,

> All the Athenians and the foreigners who lived there spent their time doing nothing but talking about and listening to the latest ideas (Acts 17:21).

Given that science and human knowledge grow precisely by the emergence of new ideas, this sounds like the right approach to me. But promoters of the gospel, in the pages of the Bible or in modern life, are not interested in sitting at the table of ideas and being subjected to the same scrutiny as all other human notions. This is because the gospel is conceived of as a supernatural message. As such, it can only be accepted or rejected. Not debated. The goal of conversion is not to win people over by facts and argumentation, but to bring about belief by an act of divine fiat—creation out of nothing. And so, from the perspective of Christianity, those who do not believe the gospel are not just coming to the wrong conclusion based on flawed reasoning. No, they are rejecting the life-transforming power of God and resisting his supernatural call to a new life. The problem is not so much that they are reasoning incorrectly, but that they are reasoning at all, and in this context, reasoning is invariably painted by evangelicals as rationalization. This is why Paul praises the foolish people of the world: they don't complicate matters with all their specious "wisdom." They just accept what he says.

Some Christian apologists and intellectuals are respectful of their interlocutors and seem to sincerely think that reasoning matters and that Christianity does have solid intellectual answers for those who are skeptical. I was one of them. But these are few and far between. For the most part, and consistent to the tradition, evangelical Christians treat unbelief as a spiritual state, and intellectual dissent as a front for moral rebellion. And even Christians who respect the intellect and deign to talk about evidence will always at some point follow the Bible's lead and bring up the question of rebellion, as, for example, when the entire philosophical enterprise is dismissed as a hopeless attempt by humans to arrive at truth without acknowledging the life-giving and mind-enlightening existence of God. It is well known that there is a culture of anti-intellectualism among evangelicals, as is perhaps the case for most popular religious movements. But my point is that this anti-intellectualism is firmly rooted in the Bible itself. Christianity as a whole, even though it does plenty of reasoning, will never be capable of embracing reason and evidence as their standard for determining truth, and it will never take people who do so seriously. This is because for Christians, belief and truth come from God, not from the observable and testable world and not from clear rational thinking. And this is why nonbelievers will always be dismissed and will always be seen as guilty of something.

FOOLS AND REBELS

After complaining about the naivete of claiming that people have control over their beliefs, I have to admit the Christian assessment of *un*belief is actually pretty sophisticated, psychologically speaking. Even on the popular level, evangelical Christians are very well versed in the psychology of denial, and can sniff out opportunities to deploy the accusation of denial with notable alacrity.

For one popular illustration, consider the 2014 film *God is not Dead*. It tells the story of a Christian college student who successfully takes on an atheist philosophy professor. The professor has, unrealistically, required all his students to sign a declaration that God is dead to pass his course. As the debate develops, the films reveals that the problem is deeper than mere ideas. The root issue is that the professor hates God due to painful experiences in his life. And when he is confronted with death, the fires of hell nipping at his heels, his defenses finally crumble, and he accepts Jesus just in time. Oops. Spoiler alert? When former Christians confess their deconversion to friends and families, the same old psychological assessments surface with notable consistency. According to evangelicals there's always some deeper personal reason why people abandoned the faith, having to do with sin, rebellion, bitterness, or bad moral influences, which crowd out any intellectual arguments or scientific evidence. This is the script, and every evangelical has a copy of it in their back pocket. The strangest aspect of it all is the incongruous experience of having people tell you that they know better than you do what is going through your own head. The only reason they think they know this is that God, who knows the minds of all people, has already told them what is happening in these situations: denial, rebellion, disobedience. Not a difference of opinion, thinking that arrives at a different conclusion, or attending to compelling evidence that contradicts the story Christianity tells about the world.

It was the Apostle Paul, again, who introduced Christians to the idea that the explanation for unbelief lies in the moral and spiritual center of the individual, not in the intellect. In Romans 1, rather than provide evidence for belief in God, he instead put forward a psychological explanation for unbelief. This is the equivalent of answering a request for evidence by saying, "It's your own fault you don't believe it." God's nature and existence are obvious from creation, Paul says, but people choose to ignore it to avoid worshiping, and therefore submitting, to him.

> For although they knew God, they neither glorified him as God nor gave thanks to him, but their thinking became futile and their foolish hearts were darkened. Although they claimed to be wise, they became fools (Romans 1:21-22).

But what is lacking here is any detailed explanation of how exactly creation points to God, and more specifically to the Christian God. The Bible as a whole, in fact, shows no interest in proving anything about God. It is rather a series of mere assertions. In the creation story, God already exists and no effort is made to explain or justify this. And rejecting him is bad by definition. Christians indulge in all manner of vilification when they are confronted with skeptics and atheists. For they are not just regular unbelievers. Atheists and skeptics have gone out of their way to challenge God. At some point, the phrase from Psalm 14:1 will make an appearance, "The fool says in his heart, 'There is no God.'" These sorts of phrases and assessments slide easily off the tongue because they are in the air that evangelicals breathe.

The influential 17th-century theologian John Calvin began his treatise on Christian theology, *The Institutes of the Christian Religion*, with the claim that the existence of the Christian God is plain to see, and humans even have a "sense of the divine" (the fancy Latin term is *sensus divinitatus*). But sin and rebellion against God get in the way of onboarding this insight. We humans, claims Calvin, just can't cross the gap of unbelief because of our self-interest. We hate God, and we don't want to bow to his authority, so we pretend he doesn't exist, and we resist the evidence that is right before our eyes. Reading Calvin as a nonbeliever is to subject yourself to an onslaught of insults. He deploys a whole thesaurus of negative terms against those who deny God. They are wicked, degenerate, absurd, blind,

GOD OF THE MIND 151

vain, rash, stupefied, bewitched, and, of course, foolish. The only way to overcome this bias, claimed Calvin, is to be "regenerated" by God. This is still essentially the Protestant evangelical view, and Calvin's ideas, which are arguably a consistent expansion of the Bible and of Paul in particular, are still today the starting point for these discussions in academic circles. The evidence is obvious, but only believers can see it. Therefore, unbelief is not a rational conclusion, but a spiritual problem. Not a morally neutral intellectual deduction, but a blameworthy denial of one's creator.

But isn't this talk about the rebellion of unbelievers just sidestepping the question? Isn't it a dysfunctional conversation in which one party changes the subject when they don't have an answer?

> *The unbeliever*: I don't believe the Bible because its entire story depends on miracles, and I don't believe in miracles.
> *The believer*: You are only saying that because you don't want God to control your life.
> *The unbeliever*: No, I'm just saying that I don't see miracles at work anywhere, and I feel like if they were real, I would. So I just don't find any miraculous account credible.
> *The believer*: Why don't you want to let Jesus in your heart? Stop resisting the Holy Spirit.
> *The unbeliever*: The only thing I'm resisting is something that doesn't make sense to me. If I thought the Bible was true, I suppose I might obey it.
> *The believer*: You are clearly hiding your resistance to God behind a bunch of rational problems. The Bible says that is foolish.
> *The unbeliever*: I'm not hiding behind anything. I'm just giving you my reasons. If you think I'm wrong, then show me why.

The believer: I will pray for you that God will open your eyes to the truth.

The notion that the unconvinced are rebellious is not too far from the logical fallacy of *ad-hominem*, where one focuses on the person who holds an opinion rather than on the opinion itself. "You only disbelieve because you are a bad person" is the fundamental claim being made once all the fancy theological terms are stripped away. All this goes a long way towards explaining why arguments about the existence of God or the truth of Christianity seem to often go around in circles with the participants talking past each other. It's because there are two completely different ways of thinking at work. In one, there is a question of logic and proof. In the other, a question of submission.

The problem of conscientious objection goes even deeper. It is not just about the right to disagree without being condemned, it is about the right to be sincerely wrong. Even if we assumed the existence of the Christian God, shouldn't an atheist be granted the courtesy of being treated as sincere? Similarly, someone who grew up in a different culture and religion might be sincere in their belief that Christianity is false—even if Christianity were true. This would seem to be a perfectly rational, not to mention courteous, possibility. But this is the specific ethical problem that Christianity can't deal with. It can't allow unbelief to be sincere. Unbelief is always bad, rebellious, and blameworthy. It lands you in hell. And God doesn't send people to hell for nothing.

But it strains credibility, psychologically speaking, to maintain that all humans who disagree with the Christian story are rebellious and blameworthy. Humans can only reason from what they know, and we should not blame someone for not knowing what they can't know, or for reasoning from the set of facts that is available to them. But Christianity does precisely this. It blames people for things that are beyond their control.

And this Christian teaching about belief and unbelief—that some beliefs are inherently blameworthy—itself becomes a point against the credibility of the Christian worldview. Supposedly, Christianity presents us with the creator's assessment of the creation. God knows how people work better than anyone else. This point is reiterated ad-nauseum in evangelical Christian circles, when it comes, for example, to issues like homosexuality, divorce, and the nature of love, sin, and holiness. God designed us, so it goes, and therefore he knows best "how we work." He knows the conditions in which humans can thrive. But then we are presented with this backward and manifestly inaccurate take on belief that is clearly a convoluted self-defense against criticism, and not based on a realistic assessment of how the human mind works. The conclusion that this is all mere human invention and not "a creator's perspective" seems difficult to avoid. These are the ideas of people. A divine perspective would be a little more sophisticated. It would at the very least be smarter than what humans can come up with. But it's pretty clear the psychology that is embedded in the Christian teaching about the ethics of belief comes to us from centuries long past and is based on ideas that have been long ago discarded by those who have spent the time and effort to study how people think and respond to the world.

 The disciple Thomas, the Christian archetype of the doubter, stated that unless he saw physical evidence of the resurrected Jesus, he would not believe. And so Jesus provided the required evidence. Thomas was able to touch Jesus' wounds and verify for himself that Jesus had indeed risen from the dead. But the account in John 20 ends with a kind of chastisement, lest there be any confusion: "You believed because you saw," says Jesus. "Blessed are those who believe without seeing." Modern people who have been schooled in the importance of using evidence and reason to determine factuality are right to ask about the rationale of this statement. Why should anyone believe anything without seeing? *And by what rationale can it be so wrong to insist on verification that one's eternal destiny hangs in the balance?* Why is God so interested in having humans assent to non-verifiable information? Surely God, the creator of the human mind, is aware that human beings have a predilection for believing all sorts of wild and crazy ideas and that the intellectual task of verification is a healthy and necessary part of the human attempt to understand the world. So why is believing without seeing put forth as a blessed condition? One explanation might be that the reasons put forward for belief are not strong enough to command the desired conclusion. And so, an alternate theory of knowledge is fabricated which facilitates the conclusion: It is praiseworthy to arrive at conclusions without evidence. In fact, to assert things which cannot be demonstrated is *superior* to mere rational or evidentiary considerations!

A more reasonable, balanced, and fair view should acknowledge the possibility that people can disbelieve ethically. That is to say that, based on what they consider in good faith to be true, they cannot accept the information embedded in the message of Christianity. To dismiss them all as being hard-hearted and rebellious is unjust, unrealistic, and downright cruel. And the idea that a person should be subjected to eternal torture with fire because they failed to arrive at the correct conclusion is downright bizarre. But let's be perfectly clear that this is explicitly entailed in Christian teaching. Hell is not just for people who behave badly. It is also for people who *think* badly.

I suppose my entire reason for undertaking this book, which I did in fits and starts, glancing nervously over my shoulder to make sure no one was reading, was to register a complaint against the cruel forces that align against people who are just trying to make sense of the world—be they curious young people, scientists studying evolution, or disaffected theologians. Fortunately, we no longer live in Galileo's Italy or in the Spanish Inquisition when the church held all the cards and rebellious thinking was swiftly silenced—sometimes around a bonfire. But somehow, incredible as it seems, the forces of orthodoxy still exert a powerful psychological control over the minds of many, through metaphysical threats and convoluted rationales. This control even spills out into culture, society, and politics—still maintaining a formidable resistance to free thought, reason, and progress.

CHAPTER 13
TRUTH WITH A CAPITAL "T"

Like many other people in the United States in 2016, I gradually became aware of the phenomenon of Donald Trump. Also like many people, I did not at first take him seriously. I thought, as I still do, that he was just a con man who liked attention, someone who will say anything to get into the spotlight. At that time, I still thought of myself as an evangelical Christian and I was sure, for the most part, my fellow evangelicals would reject Trump, since he obviously did not embody the virtues we supposedly put so much stock in. He was clearly a womanizer, a habitual liar, completely self-focused, and practiced in the art of the insult. I had lived through Bill Clinton's presidency, and I had seen, and mostly agreed with, the moral indignation that had been hurled at him for his dalliances with Monica Lewinsky. I actually liked Bill Clinton, but my mind was permanently scarred by the image of him and Monica playing with a cigar in the oval office and after that I could not take the man seriously. The fact that none of my fellow evangelicals were moved by the obvious hypocrisy of supporting Trump should have been a warning sign that the rules had changed.

I don't want to rehearse the political and social conflicts that ensued or make a list of all the irrational and non-factual claims that Trump and Trumpism unleashed on the world. That has been copiously, if not gleefully, documented. The point I want to make is very specific as it relates to my overall argument: With Trump, the sloppy deductive reasoning that is part and parcel of religion became glaringly obvious and clear for all to see. For years, I had been talking about anti-intellectualism in the church to anyone who wanted to listen. I had warned that too much of what happened in evangelicalism was simply irrational; that there was no consistency in the interpretation of the Bible, or in the application of its teachings; that people's Christian practice was often little more than superstition and credulity on display; that our view of culture was superficial, reactionary, and judgmental. And I have to say, I was weary of the battle and about to throw in the towel. I did not want to spend the rest of my days as the fringe outsider who is forever trying to hold back the madness of the crowd. But with Trump, all of these factors, which at that time I thought were only incidental to Christianity but not the core of the thing, were coming home to roost—with a vengeance. These characteristics had always been there, but restrained. Trump was like a chemical reactant. Just add a couple drops to evangelicalism and watch sloppy deduction foam up and overflow the petri dish of American religion.

NO PLACE FOR TRUTH

In the 1990s the term "postmodernism" began to circulate. It encompassed a related set of ideas that in different ways questioned the naïve objectivity embedded in modern science, philosophy, art, literature, and just about any area of learning. These critiques are still with us in many ways, even if the labeling has evolved. As with any intellectual movement, it was poorly understood among the person in the pew, and more often than not by the person in the pulpit too, and it was predictably boiled down to its most scandalous and frightening implication: "They're denying truth!" Postmodernism was for evangelicals yet another sign of the times, evidence that the secular world, after denying the God of the Bible and the Truth the Christian worldview bestowed on humanity, was increasingly descending into irrationality and chaos. But Christianity was the bulwark against such aimlessness. People need Jesus. Once they "accept the Lord" they will begin to understand the *Truth*. Sometimes a book title captures an entire mood very nicely, and such was the case with the popular tome *No Place for Truth*, written by theologian David Wells in 1993. Wells' complaint, which echoed through a series of four books on the topic, was that Western culture had become awash in subjectivity and that evangelical Protestant Christianity was being reshaped by this culture and itself becoming subjective. He was particularly critical of the fact that churches no longer taught or talked about theology. Of course, as a theologian, he would be! Churches were superficial, pastors were more like business managers than shepherds, and preaching was entertainment that catered to the issues of the day. The world had given up on *Truth*, and the church had followed suit. At the time I was a 20-something theological student who sincerely thought that the same *Truth* that Wells was trying to rescue was the solution to everything, and so I read the book with fascination, as though heeding the words of a prophet. Wells was eloquently expressing and documenting the same problems I, and others like me, had identified. If only we could get back to the *Truth* all would be well!

Evangelicals have always loved to talk about the *Truth*, and the phrase, "Truth with a capital T," is a commonplace in books, blogs, sermons, and lectures. It conveys that there is such a thing as overarching truth about the nature of the universe, what it means to be human, and how we should then live. That there is objective reality. *Truth* with a capital "t" is seen as a set of foundational ideas which ought to guide all our thinking and living. This *Truth* is not up for debate, it is something that needs to be accepted. Once you accept it, watch how it begins to make sense of your life.

The Gospel of John describes how Jesus stood before Pontius Pilate, the Roman governor of Judea, on the fateful day on which he was crucified. As the interrogation proceeds, Jesus tells Pilate: "the reason I was born and came into the world is to testify to the truth. Everyone on the side of the truth listens to me." To this Pilate responds, "What is truth?" (John 18:38). The irony in the passage is very thick (and surely engineered by the author), for in the same gospel, just a few pages earlier, Jesus declared himself to be "the way, the truth, and the life" (John 14:6). Pilate's question has become an important symbol among Christians over the centuries. It encapsulates and summarizes the world's helplessness and fallenness, its sheer blindness in the face of all the evidence. Here is Pilate, staring at *Truth* personified, and he doesn't see it. Truth, as evangelicals love to say, is a person.

All this is to say that *Truth* is for evangelicals just another word for "our religious ideas," or "all the things God told us." It's just another variation on the theme of believing, asserting, assenting, declaring things *first*, and understanding them second. Truth in evangelicalism is the beginning of the conversation. Everything flows from it, not towards it.

Carl F. Henry was in many ways the intellectual founder of modern evangelicalism. His book *The Uneasy Conscience of Modern Fundamentalism,* written in 1947, urged that conservative Christianity in the United States had abrogated its duty to be socially active. Henry called for renewed engagement with the world. Secular people might have wished that fundamentalists had stayed safely tucked away in their anti-science and anti-progress ghettos. But alas, this was not to be. Henry was well educated and conversant in the language of historical, theological, and philosophical disputation, so he could duke it out, or at least seem like he was duking it out, with the best thinkers of the day. As founder and editor of *Christianity Today*, the magazine of record for American evangelicalism, he guided and formed the movement. His five-volume theological treatment of the state of the world, called *God, Revelation and Authority*, published between 1976 and 1981, set the pattern for serious intellectual engagement with the world on the part of educated evangelicals.

Henry's *Revelation* is the same thing as Wells' *Truth*. The message is that the world has strayed from the magisterial Word of God, which gives meaning to humankind. No other system of thought provides the same level of coherence and big picture meaning that the Judeo-Christian revelation does, and all other attempts at providing meaning are both futile and sinfully misguided. They can only lead to further darkness, hopelessness, and nihilism. Henry takes on everyone: Marxism, pragmatism, logical positivism—any and all isms fall to the stroke of his pen, and all the notable thinkers get a mention. You can't accuse Henry of being uninformed. His essential claims nicely sum up some of the problems with evangelical Christian thought that have obscured my own mind for many years and which I've been highlighting and bemoaning up to this point. They provide a kind of summary of where we have been, and set the stage for my final and, dare I hope, climactic point.

Henry thinks there are two main sources of knowledge about God. First, he claims humans have knowledge of God that is innate and does not come from any experience (the philosophical term for this is *a priori* knowledge). We have already seen that this was taught by 16th-century theologian John Calvin, and Henry shows how most significant thinkers throughout Christian history have claimed something similar. He dedicates his first volume to this point, claiming that the "theological transcendent *a priori*" is the best explanatory theory of knowledge. The second source of knowledge for Henry is historical revelation, namely, the Bible. God, according to him, has revealed himself in the supernatural acts recorded in the Christian scriptures, and also in the divinely inspired ideas that are there expounded: the nature of God, sin, salvation, and eternal destiny, to name a few. He dedicates the next three volumes of his magnum opus to this topic. An important point here is that revelation, unlike *a priory* knowledge, is not something humans can access. Revelation comes straight from the mind of God, and it tells us things no human could ever investigate or deduce. As Henry says,

> All merely human affirmations about God curl into a question mark. We cannot spy out the secrets of God by obtrusive curiosity. Not even theologians of a technological era, not even Americans with their skill in probing the surface of the moon, have any special radar for penetrating the mysteries of God's being and ways. Apart from God's initiative, God's act, God's revelation, no confident basis exists for God-talk.[1]

I can personally attest that this sort of discourse can be convincing just by its sheer rhetorical energy, which propels it like a perpetual motion machine: *Truth about who we are and where we came from must come from outside of ourselves; we cannot define our own meaning into existence; only our creator can provide the framework in which being human makes sense and can be seen to have transcendental meaning. Jesus doesn't just save your soul, he also saves your mind, for without Jesus, the world becomes little more than sand sifting through our hands. All meaning is lost, as we stray through Nietzsche's "infinite nothing." But God is "the other." He is outside the universe and cannot be deduced from it. And so, God must speak to us. Revelation must be handed down. In the same way, we can't climb a ladder to heaven. A really long ladder just gets us to outer space. Getting to God is an entirely different thing altogether. That's why science can never prove God. It only works in the this-worldly sphere. But God inhabits a different plane of existence.*

Science and reason are forever condemned to traffic in the minutia of everyday factoids, but not in Revelation or Truth.[2]

But a perpetual motion machine doesn't really exist. I found this fact disappointing as a kid because I had several cool ideas that foundered on that exact point. All these grand claims are really, and at bottom, nothing more than wishful thinking. They are compelling statements, ideas found to be convincing by some, concepts that have been foundational to society for centuries, principles by which many live their lives. They are all these things and more, but that is not by any stretch of the imagination the same thing as being factual or provable. To the contrary, proof is heedlessly denied by proponents of revelation, as if by some sleight of hand, at the same time that hegemonic *Truth* is affirmed. The lack of demonstrability becomes a hallmark of its supra-human sourcing. Of course, we can't prove it! That shows it could only have come from a divine source! But if you have to accept something that cannot *by definition* be proven, demonstrated, or confirmed in any way, you have no good reason to accept it as true. There is simply nothing to go on. This is not my wacky idea, or my own idiosyncratic analysis of the situation. This is part and parcel of the evangelical Christian view of knowledge, and it is an intractable self-contradiction in the evangelical worldview, for it is claimed that Christianity demands that its adherents affirm with a great deal of conviction things which by its own account cannot be demonstrated to be true.

Not all Christian thinkers are either sophisticated or bold enough to admit this is the case. But one of the greatest, if not the greatest, contemporary defenders of Christianity, philosopher Alvin Plantinga, says as much. After all his philosophizing and cogitation, the most Plantinga can say about the truth of Christianity is that belief in God is warranted *if Christianity is true*. That's not exactly a ringing endorsement. Some evangelical Christians have complained that all his philosophizing was not, in the end, that useful to the average Christian who is struggling with doubts. Here's how Plantinga puts it:

> I won't argue that Christian belief *is* true, although I of course believe that it is. The fact is that there are some very good arguments for theistic beliefs, arguments about as good as philosophical arguments get; nevertheless, these arguments are not strong enough to support the conviction with which serious believers in God do accept theistic belief; furthermore, I don't believe that these arguments are sufficient to confer *knowledge* on one who accepts belief in God as their basis…. This is because they have warrant only if they are true; and while I think they are true, I don't think it is possible to show, by way of arguments that commend themselves to everyone, that they are. (I do believe that there are strong arguments for their truth; but these arguments are not strong enough to confer knowledge on someone who accepts them by way of these arguments).[3]

Plantinga's narrow concern is to counter the claim from many non-Christians that Christianity is irrational. He claims to show that it is in fact not irrational at all if you accept that it is true. But proving that something is rational (that it makes sense, or that it is not self-contradictory) is not by any means the same thing as showing that it is *real*. Any good fiction novel is rational in the sense that the narrative is coherent to the reader and does not contradict itself. No one thinks that it is thereby true, factual, or historical. Internal consistency is not the hallmark of factuality. The hallmark of factuality is that something really happened or really existed. You and I could drink a six-pack together and spin out dozens of rational accounts of the universe that are extremely unlikely to be true. But evangelicals often trample on this distinction with glee, ignore the fundamental question of factuality, and focus all their energies on the greatness of their message. For the believer, it is enough to show that something makes sense. Whether it is real or can be demonstrated to be real is less interesting. Kudos to Plantinga for being clear-headed and honest about this. But I think his honesty puts him out of step with most evangelicals and probably with most Christians. They, like the Carl Henrys and David Wells of the world, only want to focus their energies on extrapolating things from the *Truth*. Factuality is not as interesting, probably because there is nothing sure that can be said about the factuality of the Bible and Christianity.

EVIDENCE THAT DEMANDS SKEPTICISM

On one hand, revelation cannot be proved. On the other hand, a rational system of belief shies away from complete subjectivity and those who hold treasured beliefs are not truly satisfied with throwing up their hands and saying, "You just gotta believe." The mind reaches for at least a rationale, even if it might not be definitive. And so, among intellectually minded and educated evangelicals there are two approaches to dealing with this, or two different theories of "apologetics," the branch of theology tasked with the intellectual defense of the faith. First, there are the evidentialists, who do think you can prove revelation. Well, that's not exactly it. The specific revelatory content of the Bible can't be proven, but they claim to show God must exist, that God must be the God of the Bible, and that the Bible must be the words of that same deity. There's a lot to prove here, and not everyone is convinced. But the main point is about the reliability of the Bible. If you can show the Bible is supernaturally sourced, then it suggests the Bible is the word of God, and we can trust it to tell us things about God—to give us revelation.

However, this approach is doomed to failure. The main problem is that it's impossible to show the Bible is anything other than a book written by ancient religious people.

Miracles. The Bible describes miracles, sure. But we've

already seen that even today, where a miracle is claimed, it is extremely difficult to show that a miracle really happened. The problem becomes much more difficult when we are talking about ancient miracle reports. All we truly have as evidence of the miracles described in the Bible is the mere fact that an ancient religious text says they happened. This is not much to go on. We can't go back and ask critical questions or interview the participants. The authors of the Bible use miracles to prove their view of God, while at the same time expressing frustration, as we have seen in chapter five, at God's lack of activity. That's not exactly a recipe for objectivity. And do these miracle descriptions come from eyewitness testimony? The provenance of most of the books of the Bible is murky at best. It would be nice if there was some ancient Mesopotamian, Greek, or Roman texts that also described things like the parting of the Red Sea, the miraculous (if genocidal) battle of Jericho in which the walls of the city crumble by the power of God, or the resurrection of Jesus. But there is no such thing. If it is difficult to determine whether any miracles happen today, it is even more difficult to determine whether they happened thousands of years ago.

Prophecies. Another area of so-called proofs of the Bible's divine source is prophetic pronouncements in the Old Testament which are fulfilled in the New. However, the authors of the New Testament take a great deal of liberty with what they call a prophecy in the Old Testament, and what they call a fulfillment in the New. Here are some examples in Matthew:

- *Matthew 1:22-23* claims Mary's divine impregnation, with Jesus, was a fulfillment of Isaiah, "The virgin will be with child and will give birth to a son, and they will call him Immanuel." But the prophecy in Isaiah does not imply, as Matthew does, and as our English translations encourage, that the woman was a virgin, only a young woman of marriageable age. Further, the prophecy in Isaiah is pitched to the

prophet's own time, but the prophetic genre, which is expansive and majestic, allows for flexibility of interpretation.
- *Matthew 2:23* says that Jesus moved to Nazareth to fulfill the prophecy, "he shall be called a Nazarene." But this is not mentioned anywhere in the Bible.
- *Matthew 13:35* claims that Jesus taught in parables to fulfill what it says in Psalm 78:2: "I will open my mouth in parables, I will utter hidden things." This is hardly a miraculous fulfillment. It is not even presented as a prophecy, but is rather the introduction to what follows in the Psalm itself.

There are also bound to be congruencies that stem from the fact that Jesus was himself steeped in the Hebrew Scriptures and probably saw himself described in them (see Luke 24:27). At times he even performed symbolic actions that alluded to the scriptures, as, for example, when he instructs his disciples to acquire a donkey and rides it into Jerusalem (Mark 11:1-10), to suggest Zechariah 9:9: "See your king comes to you…gentle and riding on a donkey, on a colt, the foal of a donkey." Finally, the fact that prophetic fulfillments are necessarily recorded after the predictions and by people who were looking for fulfillments needs to be factored in. There is nothing about biblical prophecy that compels us to conclude it was done by God. Humans could have very easily and very reasonably done all of it.

The Bible is insightful. Showing that the Bible is very wise, insightful, or that it has served as the basis of important civilizations for over two thousand years does not prove that its metaphysical claims about God are accurate, nor does it in any way verify them. Why do we need to say anything more than that the Bible is the product of ancient religious authors? Human beings are capable of being wise and insightful on their own, and without miraculous intervention. What is more likely? That ancient religious authors came up with some ideas about God to explain their world? Or that God revealed himself in such a way that it is hard to distinguish his revelation from the ideas of ancient authors who were trying to make sense of the world?

The Bible is historically accurate. Evangelicals delight in being told about the historical background of the Bible, and in hearing about historical research that independently confirms the context of some of its stories. It is as if showing that the Bible really was written by ancient people who lived in ancient cultures proves that its claims about God are also true. How does that follow? We've already established that nothing can confirm or deny what God says about himself (if he has said anything). Proving that some guy who was supposedly inspired by God really did live in the 6th century BCE does not in any way prove he was speaking on behalf of an entity that cannot be demonstrated to exist.

What the Bible says about itself. The worst defense is the one that quotes the Bible's own assertions about its own validity. Clearly, relying on a narrator's own assertions about his own contested testimony lacks credibility. The problem is that there is little else to go on. How can anything in history prove God has spoken? The Bible says it is the word of God spoken to Abraham, Moses, Elijah, Isaiah, Jeremiah, Jesus, and the Apostles Peter, John, and Paul. In 2 Timothy 3:16 there is the claim that all scripture is God-breathed. Can we get someone else to confirm this? Of course not. No one can observe God-breathing-ness. Only God himself can, if he exists, tell us he inspired the Bible. If we knew another god who could corroborate 2 Timothy 3:16, that would be helpful. But we don't.

Coherence. Much is made by evangelicals about the fact that the Bible is a collection of 66 distinct books that were written over a period of about a thousand years by many different authors, and that, lo and behold, they all teach the same thing! Isn't that amazing? How could that have happened without divine intervention? Quite easily, it turns out. This claim is a dishonest misconstrual, since the books of the Bible all form part of an evolving tradition where each contribution builds on the ideas and insights of former authors. It's not as if the authors of the books of the Bible were sequestered from each other and just so happened to come up with the same ideas without any dialog. Clearly, the newer books of the Bible depend on the older ones, as can be seen by frequent citations, references to previously described events, and the attempts at demonstrating prophetic fulfillment. Additionally, there is nothing clearly miraculous about the formation of the canon of Scripture. On one hand, there are several different Bibles in several different Christian traditions. On the other hand, what little we do know about the decisions to include or exclude books from the Bible comes down to very human debates that don't require divine agency to be explained. Basically, at different times, different religious leaders argued for or against including different books in the Bible.

The resurrection of Jesus is the crowning argument of evidential apologetics. This is the single most amazing and provable, they say, miracle of all, and the one which the Bible itself claims must be true. For, "if Christ has not been raised, your faith is futile" (1 Corinthians 15:17). Many books have been written for and against the proposition that the resurrection of Jesus is a historically verifiable event. For our purposes, I'll just reiterate that the problem with historical miracles applies as much here as anywhere else. Let me put it this way: What is more likely, that a group of religious people two thousand years ago became convinced their leader had risen from the dead when he had not, or that a real person literally came back to life with a physical/spiritual body? Religious gullibility is something that can be observed, documented, and confirmed every day. People coming back to life after being actually dead cannot be. It seems reasonable, therefore, to go with the first option. I think if the question could be posed neutrally, without bringing religious commitment to bear, most people would agree. Unfortunately, claims about the supernatural tend to be cloaked in religious ideas and religious commitments.

THE BEST OF ALL POSSIBLE EXPLANATIONS

So much for evidentialism. Let's turn our attention to the other approach to defending the truth of Christianity—presuppositionalism. Don't be afraid of the name. It's actually a simple concept. Instead of attempting to show factuality, this approach assumes that something is true and then proves it, or at least demonstrates that it is likely, by showing that it makes the most sense of the world and of the human condition.

I was first exposed to this approach through the famous apologist and thinker Francis Shaeffer. Based in Switzerland, sporting a hip goatee, and dialoging with all the great thinkers of the day—there was an air of the exotic about him, and it was inevitable that I would join the fan club, even if belatedly. He died in 1984, before I was even aware of his work. I myself took to wearing a goatee, inspired by Schaeffer, and was elated when my friends told me I looked like him. Schaeffer's very definite presuppositional position was that, after years of poring over all the great religions and great ideas humans have offered up to explain how we came here and where we are going, Christianity is the only possible answer. Not, he would emphatically clarify, the *best* answer, but the *only* possible answer to the question of life, the universe, and everything. He took this up in two different categories. First, he claimed there was a philosophic necessity, a question or series of questions that demanded an answer: Why does anything exist at all? Schaeffer claimed the biblical doctrine of creation was the only good answer. The second was something he called "the mannishness of man," a phrasing that has not aged well and could have just as well been labeled "the humanness of humanity," or simply human nature. The lived experience of people, claimed Shaeffer, was itself a kind of witness to human origins because we humans assume things and long for things that (it just so happens) Christianity gives us.

I remember hearing him on this latter point in a memorable recorded lecture that I replayed many times in the early 1990s. Here Schaeffer claimed that Sigmund Freud, who thought romantic love was just an expression of repressed sexuality, nevertheless valued romance and told his fiancé in a letter to love him irrationally. For Schaeffer, this was tragic, because here are human beings who are trying to live out their God-given purpose in the world while at the same time denying God's existence and his revealed truth. And doing this, he claimed, will generate profound contradictions. But Christianity must be true, he maintained, because it explains the why and how of human nature, and provides, if we will only submit to it, a guide to life that is both intellectually and experientially satisfying. Love, Schaeffer would say, comes from God, who is himself the ultimate example of love. And since humans have been made in his image, we share intuitions, even if they are sometimes only vaguely apprehended, of that divine love.

But even if it is true that one interpretation of life is more satisfying or coherent than others, does this really prove anything? The question is not what is more satisfying or what makes more sense, but what is factual. The real world of facts is not necessarily satisfying and does not necessarily cohere into a grand meaningful narrative. The question of factuality must be determined with tools designed to determine factuality, not on the basis of subjective factors. It would be nice if philosophy and theology were a little more like physics, where there is a theoretical branch which is allowed to indulge in flights of speculative fancy. But theoretical physics, in order to become actual science, must pass the crucible of experimental physics. There has to be a prediction that can be tested and seen to be true by the scientific community. Only then does theoretical physics become physics in the true sense. This distinction is unfortunately lost on many lay people and perhaps even on many science reporters who, when they hear or report on some new esoteric theory of, say, how the universe was formed, fail to even wonder about experimental confirmation, making it seem like physicists just sit around coming up with strange and wonderful ideas. Perhaps one reason for this lack of awareness of the importance of experimental verification is that we humans are accustomed to judging theories about life simply on the basis of how intuitive they sound, and little more. And the problem with theological explanations of the world is that there will never, by definition, ever be any "experimental verification" of those ideas. Theological explanations will always have a "seems like" kind of verification process. One of the pieces that is surprisingly absent from Schaeffer's bold claim that Christianity is the best explanation is any consideration of how to determine what is best or worst. What are the principles we can use to determine what system of thinking makes the most sense? Is there a scale of some sort? How does each religion or philosophy score? The reason there is no such thing is that each religion and each philosophical system would inevitably come up with its own unique scale, based on its own unique principles and concerns.

There is another problem with Schaeffer's claim that Christianity just so happens to match up, at least in the mind of many, with our deepest human aspirations and provide an explanatory framework for our behavior and the universe we inhabit. It's the age-old question of the chicken and the egg. What came first, the universe and our experience of it or the explanation? Is the reason Christianity seems to explain the experience of being human simply that it is a story crafted by humans? Similarly, a dog's theology might try to account for why dogs love to chase balls thrown by humans by arguing that humans have obviously created both dogs and balls to perfectly complement each other (a dog heretic, however, might aver that dogs also like to chase cats and rabbits). Clearly, human explanations of the world *will make sense of the world to humans*! To point out the amazing confluence between explanation and phenomena proves nothing other than what humans are and what they think. How could we ever tell the difference between something we made up to explain the world and an explanation of the world from the outside? As we have seen, God always talks through people, and the only difference between explanations of the world is, materially speaking, simply that people say different things. But it's always people. Saying things.

Because of all this, the presuppositional approach to proving the truth of Christianity, the Bible, and God amounts to little more than leaning into confirmation bias. Practitioners of a particular religion will think that following its precepts will make the most sense. How could it be otherwise? Believing first is a powerful motivator. It forms your mind and your emotions. Religion creates a social reality and patterns individuals to that reality such that its interpretative scheme becomes intuitively desirable. And even people who are only lightly touched by a religious worldview can still be prone to a sense that it seems likely to be true when they are exposed to a more detailed exposition. But none of this amounts to anything that can ever truly be verified. In fact, the opposite is true: The fact that religious notions cannot be verified but "seem to be true" becomes a source of muddled and unclear thinking. Religious adherents know they make the most fundamental decisions about the meaning of life based on whether things *seem to be true*, not on the basis of disciplined observation of the world. The conclusion that disciplined observation of the world is only of limited value is bound to resonate. Once a religious tradition develops into a fully-fledged worldview spanning centuries and civilizations, its truthfulness is seemingly embedded into life itself because its ideas have already had a formative effect on culture and society. To then recognize that these ideas are the "best explanation" proves only that they are the explanations that we have already accepted, and nothing more than that.

And is it really all so dire, dehumanizing, and irrational to organize society without God in the center? People who cannot believe in "things unseen" might beg to differ. The decoupling of religion from politics has led to a boon in well-being. No more religious wars, no more tests of orthodoxy for political and social engagement, no more burning of heretics, no more curtailing of free speech (also known to some as heresy), no more authority figures telling us how to live our lives, and no more theologians telling scientists what they can and can't study. Of course, many Christians are still trying to do such things in the name of *Truth*. They have had some recent successes, like overturning *Roe v. Wade*, but for the most part their enthusiasm is held back by a secular constitution and set of laws that are based not on *Truth*, but on equal treatment of everyone regardless of their religious beliefs or lack of them. I for one am quite happy with this situation. It seems that many others are as well. And is that secular approach to society "true" in some sense? I wouldn't dare to say that. But how society is organized is not primarily a question of truth. It is a question of convenience. It is something we humans decide in dialog with each other. That is all it is and that is all it needs to be.

Many people think Christianity is a great idea. And just the mere act of thinking it is a great idea seems to make it real. But listen closely and you will see that behind all the intellectual, often well-informed, and highly complex theological assessments of the state of the world by evangelicals and all their proffered solutions, there lies an intractable subjectivity: You can't prove any of it by any conceivable means. Because of this, proof itself is subjected to critique and obfuscation. "Mere proof!" scoffs the theologian. "Only faithless intellectuals who have been corrupted by modern philosophy demand proof. You can't prove God. You can only accept that He has spoken—and obey."

There is no doubt that Christianity is a rational religion. Christians have been defending the rationality of their worldview for two thousand years, and entire libraries are filled with their often dense and sophisticated theological disputations. That point is often missed by its detractors, who treat Christianity, and evangelicalism in particular, as uninformed superstition. That's not exactly fair. But the point Christians themselves often miss is that all that rational discourse is built on a subjective foundation. You can't prove revelation. That's axiomatic. That leaves you with just accepting it, and there's no other option. And since this revelation comes to us through the writings of ancient religious people, this opens the door to the obvious observation that what is called revelation might just as well be the writings of ancient religious people and nothing more.

CHAPTER 14
THE POST TRUTH WORLD

As we settled into the bizarre world of Donald Trump's presidency, I kept wondering how it could be that people who are so obsessed with *Truth* could even put up with that man. For me, it was a gut level rejection. I can't stand being around people who are so clearly manipulating facts to get their way. I had a friend in high school who was cut from the same cloth. His conversation, if it can be called that, was a continual drivel of lies and half-truths that were obviously engineered to impress me. The pressure I felt to *be* visibly impressed, when in fact I was just annoyed and irritable, was exhausting. This guy was making up his own story as he went along, and no amount of skepticism or fact-checking could hold back the narrative. We haven't kept in touch. For those who fall for this sort of truth-defying self-aggrandizement, Trump is like a god.

THE MAGA TURN

Trump also understood that he could say anything he wanted and make any claim he wanted, as long as it supported the worldview of his base. He, in effect, understood one of the main arguments of my book: People accept big ideas first. Once that happens, you can tell them anything that supports the big ideas, and they will accept, believe, or at the very least go along with those claims, no matter how petty or absurd. As Trumpism blossomed, a strange thing happened: the secular, liberal establishment began to fret about truth and objectivity, with phrases like "post-truth world" and "alternative facts," grabbing national attention, garnering commentary, and serving as fodder for memes. Meanwhile, evangelicals, the self-appointed guardians of *Truth*, descended into the murky swamp of manufactured reality and visibly embraced the postmodern subjectivity they had been decrying for decades, wielding *Truth* as a cynical weapon for political control.

In response to this onslaught of the incoherent, I began to make a distinction in my thinking and conversations between truth and facts. This was new for me. Up to that point, I was operating under the impression that the term "truth" had a secular definition, one which all parties agreed on. Namely, truth as "that which is in accordance with reality." But when truth becomes *Truth*, that definition stops working, because now the conflict over methods of truth-seeking have become embedded in the word itself. Those who believe first think their religious ideas are "that which is accordance with reality." They think belief in a revealed creed is how we get to the nature of reality. But those who have a secular approach based on observation think attending to the brute facts of the world is how we arrive at truth. Because of this, the term truth is essentially useless. It hides the most important epistemological question within itself and sows confusion such that people are saying the same word but meaning completely different things. When religious people say "truth" they mean "what God said" (which is literally what a bunch of ancient religious writers said). When secular, scientifically informed people say "truth," they mean "the facts of the matter as can be determined by observation." And evangelical support for Trump, along with that whole universe of misinformation, conspiracy theories, and downright insane claims, showed in the most public way possible that the evangelical version of *Truth* has little to no interest in facts. It's all *Truth* and no place for truth.

Evangelicals were so accustomed to reasoning from their big picture heavenly principles down to the earth that they transferred this seamlessly into the secular realm. It used to be that the devil was the bad guy. But now it was the liberals. Evangelicalism was co-opted to become a political vessel when the idea that liberalism will ruin the world achieved the status of "capital T Truth." After that, facts were no longer relevant, and all the dynamics I have been highlighting in this book came into play. Believe first, understand second. Once you know the Truth, you no longer have to thoroughly explore the facts of the matter. Once an idea becomes foundational, everything and anything proves it. Any claims that support the big idea are immediately and intuitively credible on a visceral level. Maybe they are believable and maybe they are not. But they are certainly *repeatable*. Anything that illustrates the *Truth* is true enough.

Listening to Trump and his supporters during the unfolding of their "Big Lie" that the election was stolen was strangely reminiscent of the sorts of things that I used to hear in church: misconstrual, special pleading, and explanations that only make sense if you squint hard. These are things that work not because of their inherent worth, but because people want them to work.

- The election must have been stolen because Trump was ahead in the counting at some point, but later Joe Biden surged ahead. Clearly, this proves nothing. Unless you want it to prove something.
- The size of Trump rallies in Georgia proved Biden could not have won the state. That it proves nothing of the sort is completely obvious, starting with the

assumption that just because someone attends a rally their vote is predetermined.
- The affirmation that there is evidence to prove everything, but the evidence never quite surfaces. Rudy Giuliani and Sidney Powell, for example, repeatedly claimed they had evidence of fraud, or were about to obtain it, but it never materialized. Giuliani even told Rusty Bowers, then speaker of the Arizona House, that he would send him the evidence right away. He never did.
- Strange and unlikely interpretations of laws and legal procedures. The pressure put on Pence to stop certification of electoral votes is a perfect example. Most people have no idea what the law says about this procedure, and many people would not even be able to understand the relevant text. Similar to the Bible, legal documents can be difficult for lay people to interpret, and so one must take the word of one's favorite "preacher."
- Trump's ability to be convincing, at least to his acolytes, without any reference to confirming data. Just say things the right way, and people will believe and follow. The shocking fact is that the one and only source of the claim of a stolen election was the words of Donald Trump. For evangelicals, accepting the mere word of a charismatic speaker is par for the course. They do it every Sunday.

For me, the most memorable character in the drama of the Big Lie was Eric Metaxas, an evangelical intellectual turned Trumpism adherent. I suppose the reason he is memorable is that I understand where he came from, since it is where I myself came from. But I'm shocked at where he ended up. We inhabit completely different universes now. He famously declared that he was willing to die in the fight to keep Trump in power. The fact that he is still with us and that Trump's Big Lie did not succeed suggests he could have tried a little harder. I had read Eric's 2011 book *Bonhoeffer: Pastor, Martyr, Prophet, Spy* about Dietrich Bonhoeffer, a German pastor who resisted Hitler and the Nazis and was eventually executed for it. I enjoyed it, even if I was aware that Metaxas was trying too hard to make his subject seem like an evangelical. Metaxas is deeply steeped in the history of Germany during the rise and reign of Hitler, and he regularly points to parallels between those times and current politics. What struck me as odd was that here was a person who is very well-informed about the rise to power of the most famous and consequential of all fascists,[1] someone who admires those who resisted Hitler to the death, yet he somehow decided to support Donald Trump, the leader of a movement that has, objectively speaking, all the marks of fascism. The incoherence is mind-numbing. At a prayer meeting on December 2, 2020, almost a month into the Big Lie, Metaxas made a statement at the "Global Prayer for U.S. Election Integrity"[2] that nicely sums up my entire point about what happens when religious, faith-based reasoning makes the leap into politics. At this time, Trump had been claiming, without any evidence, that the election was stolen. But this did not faze Metaxas. He is used to believing in things that cannot be demonstrated, and he knows that doubts don't come from lack of factuality, but from spiritual forces.

> If we're going through a time of darkness where in the natural world we're not getting the evidence—or whatever—we need, there is no doubt that we must stand firm. It's like somebody saying, 'Oh, you don't have enough evidence to believe in Jesus.' We have enough evidence in our hearts. We know him and the enemy is trying harder than anything we have seen in our lives to get us to roll over, to forget about it.[3]

This is why no amount of fact-checking ever dented support

for Trump. It was never about facts. It's about *Truth*. The battle in the heavens has spilled out into earthly politics. Like my friend in high school, politically activated evangelicals were, and still are, making up their own story as they go along, weaving the continual stream of culturally available information into their grand narrative. If something seems confirming, it confirms. If something seems contrary, it is the work of "the devil." Metaphorically. In fact, the liberals. A political movement that is based on authority, that is morally self-righteous, and has little interest in the facts of the matter is a great fit for evangelicals. This is the religious mental model evangelicals have been trained in from day one.

It's tempting to say that conservative politicians brilliantly and cynically figured out how to co-opt the religious brain for political purposes. But the story might be more complicated: Maybe it was the conservative evangelical brain, with forebearers going back to the revolutionary period, that created conservative politics in the first place. And maybe it was secular conservatives who didn't realize their ideas were unsustainable without certain *Truths* to back them up. Only, it's taken until now for this to become completely obvious. The thoughtful conservatives who cannot stomach Trumpism have jumped ship and found that they have much more in common with many liberals, simply because they share a common epistemology. I may disagree with you, but if we both hate liars, cheats, and fascists, we'll have a great time together trash-talking them.

THERE'S NO DEMOCRACY IN HEAVEN

It should come as no surprise that a system of thought and life based on believing unprovable things because they were supposedly handed down from an authoritative source will tend to take the side of authority and authoritarians in the real world. When Christianity gets into positions of power, it inevitably sides with authority. How could it not? German Lutherans supported Hitler, Pope Pius XI helped Mussolini come to power, the Russian Orthodox church loves Putin, and American evangelicals worship Trump. The Bible looks forward to a day when Jesus will rule the nations with a rod of iron (Psalm 2:7-9, Revelation 19:15). As evangelicals themselves can be heard to quip, heaven is not a democracy. Even evangelicals who support democracy acknowledge that it is just a temporary arrangement, for in a universe that is run by the God of the Bible, authoritarianism is the nature of reality itself. Christianity did not invent democracy. That was the Greeks. Nor did democracy make any advances during the thousand years that Christianity had the run of Europe. During that period, birthright monarchy was the rule of the land and the only caveat the church made to this arrangement was to insist that the church's authority superseded the authority of kings, for the pope was the representative of God on earth. You can't go any higher than that. Modern democracy was crafted by enlightenment figures who went out of their way to curb the destructive influence of religion by decoupling it from political power.

Of course, not all evangelicals run headlong into the arms of fascists and authoritarians. For example, Rusty Bowers, mentioned above, was himself a Christian and he did not give in to the lies of Trump and his team. Those who resist over-reaches of power in the name of God and Christian ideals have a robust tradition of "speaking truth to power" in the prophetic books of the Hebrew Bible. And while much good has certainly come from this, it is important to remember the prophetic tradition still operates firmly within the authoritarian model. The problem the prophets rail against is the failure of kings to adhere to and impose the laws of God, who is the ultimate authority. While some of their social principles regarding how to treat the poor, for example, can be universally applauded, we should not forget that adherence to the God of Israel is an unquestioned pillar of the prophetic vision. And in their proclamations, deviation from the worship of the one true God results in destruction and violence, as we have seen.

It is no surprise, then, that as soon as an opening presents itself, people whose view of the world comes from the Bible tend to align themselves with authority figures who are willing to impose God's will on society. This is the most fundamental, basic, ideological source of evangelical support for Trump. It also explains why there was a surge in Christian nationalism under his presidency, and that challenges to the notion of separation of church and state are becoming louder and louder, finding support even among members of Congress.

Certainly, many evangelical Christians defend historical liberalism, democracy, and the separation of church and state. American democracy arguably owes a debt to the Quakers, a Christian sect that focused on Jesus' pacifist teachings and was behind the founding of Pennsylvania, and that influenced American ideals about equality. But these more progressive Christians are out of step with the bulk of the teachings of the Bible, to say nothing of basic religious tribalistic instincts. Christians who value freedom of religion, the right to privacy, minority rights, and political self-determination don't have any verses. These are principles which can be extrapolated from the Bible if one has the will to engage in such a task, but they are not the core of the thing.

Bible verses that don't exist:

- And he will rule the nations as a duly elected official.
- Those who worship other gods will peacefully recline with Christians and live together in a shared kingdom of peace forever.
- The foreigner among you shall be allowed to live however they see fit.
- And the Lord will rejoice in people's free self-expression and delight in allowing humans to live

however the hell they want, so long as it does not harm anyone else.

No, there is nothing even remotely like this in the Bible, for it is a book that unequivocally demands obedience on all levels of human experience and can only envision peace and harmony in a world where the conditions of obedience are perfectly met. And when evangelical Christians want to show that America was "founded on Christian values" they don't go to Quaker Pennsylvania to prove their point, but to Puritan New England. These pilgrims set out explicitly to found a new religious monoculture in which everyone lived and believed the same way. Those who did not conform were demoted and ostracized, and the Native Americans were "Canaanites" to be destroyed. The Puritans had all the good verses. Verses we *can* find in the Bible:

- "Before me every knee will bow; by me every tongue will swear. They will say of me, 'In the Lord alone are righteousness and strength.'" All who have raged against him will come to him and be put to shame (Isaiah 45:23-24).
- "At the name of Jesus every knee should bow, in heaven and on earth and under the earth, and every tongue confess that Jesus Christ is Lord" (Philippians 2:10-11).
- "Therefore go and make disciples of all nations, baptizing them in the name of the Father and of the Son and of the Holy Spirit, and teaching them to obey everything I have commanded you" (Matthew 28:18-20).
- "In the cities of the nations the LORD your God is giving you as an inheritance, do not leave alive anything that breathes…Otherwise, they will teach you to follow all the detestable things they do in worshiping their gods" (Deuteronomy 20:16, 18).

Clearly, the religious vision of Christianity is that of total and complete compliance by every single human being, with no quarter given to religious freedom, freedom of conscience, freedom of speech, or any other related freedoms. This is not even controversial. It's the endgame. The near game is a little less clear. Some evangelicals think the job of Christians is just to "preach the gospel" for now, and to stay out of politics. But the totalitarianism of the future keeps slipping back into the present, simply because the rationality and rhetoric of Scripture seem to demand it. The words, phrases, and ideas are there, and they are too easy to deploy, even if a more sophisticated theological assessment might argue otherwise.

JESUS IS THE ANSWER

The idea that humans will ever completely agree about metaphysics and morality is absurd. This is precisely why secular society was invented. Secularism is the only solution to the problem of pluralism: Everyone gets to believe and act according to the dictates of their own conscience, so long as their actions do not harm others. Religion is relegated to the private sphere. Those who wish to live as adherents of a particular religion or sect are free to do so. Those who do not wish to associate with any religion at all are also free to do so, and the state has nothing to say about this one way or another. That's a good solution, and it really works. The problem is that religious people, evangelicals in particular, are never completely on board with the secular principle. It can seem like they are when culture generally favors their moral vision, but when the mismatch between the religious worldview and the secular worldview passes a certain threshold, evangelicals will set secularism aside and try to reassert a religious monoculture. This is exactly what is happening today in the United States. It explains why important personal and moral questions like abortion, gender identity, and sexuality have entered the political sphere, and why so many evangelicals are bent on "reclaiming our nation for God," promoting public expressions of Christian faith, and trying to get Christian ideas and their implications enacted into law. The big surprise in the last few years has been just how many people are still holding out for this religious monoculture, how vociferous they are, and the extent to which they are willing to go.

When I was a Christian, I thought the solution to all the problems of the world was the love of God which changes hearts through grace. Was there apartheid in South Africa? They need Jesus. Was there political strife in Northern Ireland? They need the love of God. Was there genocide in Rwanda? Jesus. Was there irrational hatred against Westerners in the Middle East? If only Muslims could acknowledge that Jesus Christ is Lord, all their strife would cease. But even as I relished this vision, there was always a question mark hovering: The idea that everyone would convert to Christianity seemed a bit unrealistic, and that result isn't even envisioned by the Bible. According to Scripture, there will always be a rebellious majority that does not submit to Jesus and goes to hell. So why, I wondered, am I offering such a practical sounding but completely unrealistic solution? The love of God can't be the solution because most people won't accept it. That won't help anyone in the real world anyway. If I wanted to solve problems today, it seemed, I had to deal with the permanent reality of religious dissent and pluralism. Therefore, Jesus cannot be the answer to the problems of the world today. For him to be the answer implies religious and ideological totalitarianism that only leads to strife. You can't impose love. You can only give it and hope for a return. That's all. You can't build a society on the notion that everyone will love each other or that everyone will even share a common idea of love and truth. To build such a society, you will need coercion, which is diametrically opposed to the stated goal.

Ironically, a closer look at the conflicts I thought Jesus could solve—if only he were allowed—shows that they arguably came about because of *too much* Jesus. Apartheid had a biblical rationale and came from a colonial Dutch Christian culture. The strife in Ireland involved Protestant and Catholic Christians killing each other. The Rwandan genocide took place in a region where most people identified as Christian. And whatever is happening in the Middle East at any given moment cannot be divorced from centuries of religious conflicts between Christians and Muslims. These examples (and many others) profoundly challenge the proposition that Jesus is the answer, and the answer is that he's not.

Some Christians will demur that all these hotspots had the wrong version of Jesus. Well, okay. But that raises the problem of the effectiveness of Christianity. If it is constantly being "misunderstood" such that it ends up at the center of most of the world's conflicts and violence, then that would tend to suggest it is not very effective, and calls into question the idea that God is moving it forward with the power of the Spirit. Christians know that hell is the destination of their enemies, and as we have seen, even Jesus, the great proffered answer, will preside over such eternal punishment. The leap in rationale from that ultimate reality to the destruction of this-world enemies is intuitive and close at hand. As history shows, it's a common enough move.

Jesus is not the answer. Totalitarianism is not the answer. Fascism is not the answer. Any proposal that involves the imposition of a religion or an ideology on everyone equally is not the answer. We humans don't agree on what the answer is, so we have to learn to live with multiple answers. Which is to say that we must live under the umbrella of secular pluralism. That's the answer. It's a good one, and it works, if only we can resist the impulse to interfere with it when it makes our group uneasy.

CHAPTER 15
INTELLECTUAL HUMILITY

What if we just made it all up? How would we know one way or another? Is there any real difference between revelation and fantasy? Both might just as well be the product of the human mind. How could we tell the difference? We know the mind is good at making things up, and that many people and many cultures have created impressive castles in the air, castles which come crashing down to earth when the spotlight of disciplined inquiry is shined on them. So what is it about the castle of evangelical Christianity that makes it different? What gives it a foundation that connects it solidly to the ground? Isn't revelation destined to forever remain suspended on nothing, floating in the air by magic and miracle?

My position is not that I can answer these questions definitively, be it with a yes or a no. My position is simply that no one can answer them with any level of certainty. They are unanswerable. It is implied by the nature of our existence in the physical world of cause and effect that we cannot have certainty about supernatural claims. This is even recognized by theologians and believers, even if the insight is not consistently onboarded and applied, and its implications are hidden behind a curtain of obfuscation.

I remember another strange and heretical idea coming to me while reading a section of the biblical book of Galatians. In this book, the Apostle Paul is correcting people who have listened to the wrong voices and have gone astray. They have abandoned the gospel for false teaching. But Paul tells them in no uncertain terms that since they were saved by the Gospel of Jesus, they must continue in that same gospel and must resist getting sidetracked by other competing claims. At one point he makes this surprising statement:

> Even if we or an angel from heaven should preach a gospel other than the one we preached to you, let them be under God's curse! (Galatians 1:8).

I thought the reasoning was strange, for it seems to deconstruct the entire idea that we should believe the gospel (or the Bible) because it is the revealed word of a supernatural being. Paul seems to envision the possibility that there are multiple, competing, supernatural voices, and that all you can do in the face of this plurality of supernatural claims is to keep believing the first one you heard, no matter what. But, I wondered, if you can't trust the word of a supernatural being, in this case an angel, who *can* you trust! Paul himself underwent a supernatural conversion in which he saw a bright light, and a being claiming to be Jesus spoke to him. So why does *that* get to be the supernatural revelation that goes unquestioned? Why does *that* get to be the standard upon which everything else is judged, even the messages of other supernatural beings? How could Paul possibly know which supernatural being was true and right? How does he even know whether one supernatural being is an angel or a devil? After all, the devil is also known to impersonate good beings.

The Bible itself raises, but does not deal with, the problem that humans living in the universe of cause and effect are ill-equipped to judge the veracity of any so-called supernatural revelation. Even if we took for granted the existence of a supernatural realm, we still would have no way of verifying competing claims. Humans would basically be sitting ducks for any supernatural being. Are they good or bad? Is there even such a thing as good or bad in other realms? What are the motivations of these beings? Do they have our own interests at heart, or are we pawns in a vast game we can never understand? Or are supernatural beings so different from us that we don't even understand what they are trying to tell us, even if it seems like we do? And maybe the beings themselves don't even understand *us*! The only answer people can provide to these questions is, "I know because I take the word of one supernatural being over the word of another supernatural being." That's it. There is no other possible answer, and that is no answer. So even if there is a supernatural realm, we still have no way of adjudicating any claims that come from it because all we get is what some being says about it.

THE BIG MAN HYPOTHESIS

Both atheists and theists, it seems, argue for and against one version of God, essentially the monotheistic Christian one. But even if there is an intelligence behind the creation of the universe or the origins and development of life on earth, there are still many possibilities regarding the nature, identity, and purposes of such a being. Some of those possibilities abide in a gray area between God as the supra-natural entity who created the entire cosmos and God as a highly capable and intelligent super-being or beings who abide in the universe. Or a combination thereof. Or something completely other that we are incapable of imagining. Sometimes the notion that we can sort this all out based on our current state of knowledge seems laughable and childish. Why the rush to embrace one conclusion that was crafted several thousand years ago? I am not here to say that no God exists. On the other hand, though, we don't at this juncture have anything other than pure theological speculation to go on. And instead of approaching the question with a disciplined open mind and paying attention to the facts of the matter, what we have is a bunch of salesmen peddling unlikely claims and demanding acquiescence without critical engagement. Why is anyone taking this seriously? That's the big question. It's difficult to avoid the conclusion that religion is a kind of mind virus, finely evolved to take advantage of a set of psychological defects that are baked into the human mind—because there is almost nothing outside the human mind to suggest any of these claims are factual.

The reason that both pro and con argue about the same God's existence, and the reason we have landed on this one particular "big man" God concept, is mostly that "he" is easily generated by the human imagination. He is a larger-than-life parent, an authority figure above all authority, a someone in charge who makes sense of both the world and the life and hopes and aspirations of individuals. He is the rational extrapolation of a child's experience of their parent. A parent to a grownup. Is it pure coincidence that God's qualities and attributes are all human qualities writ large?

- Humans have knowledge. God has all knowledge.
- Humans love. God's love is the purest of all.
- Humans make plans for the future. God's plans for the future are the best—and they're guaranteed!
- Humans experience injustice and are angered when dishonored. But God is more honorable than anyone, and dishonoring him is the greater insult.
- Humans have life, but it is finite. God's life is predictably endless.
- Humans have power over their environment. God's power is complete and total.

- Humans have an urge to care for smaller, weaker creatures, be they human babies or members of the animal world. God's compassion is all-encompassing.

The important question here is whether there is anything we attribute to God that is not an extrapolation of what humans are, do, and feel. Even in polytheistic religions, the gods are presented as super people, as in the ancient Greco-Roman religion, or in tribal religions. Judaism, Christianity, and Islam have affirmed the single, "one big person" God idea. But this is not categorically different. It is just a logical next step. It's tidying up the basic idea and making it more compelling, but it's still the same idea. The gods-as-bigger-people become the one God as the biggest ever person. I have heard Christian apologists talk about how the gods of the ancients were just regular people writ large, with all their flaws and relational messes, and then without any hint of irony propose that the true God of the Bible is different, for he is perfect, all powerful, and has none of the defects attributed to the Gods of polytheism. He is, in effect, a *perfect* person writ large as if this were a categorically different proposal. If flawed people are the product of the fevered ancient imagination, what are the chances that a perfect person is not a product of the same imagination? These are all ideas that strike the human mind and, due to myriad factors from culture to psychology to the geopolitical state of the world, make intuitive sense. But they are so clearly open to the criticism that they are projections of the imagination, and this should give us pause. As I have already claimed in chapter six, there is a God-figure in our minds. This does not mean that there is a God-figure in the universe that exists outside of our minds. That is an *entirely* different question, one which is fraught with problems.

Theists have answers to the claim that God is a psychological projection. They point out that just because you can imagine something, that doesn't mean that it's not true. But we have *seen* humans and we know they are really good at imagining things. We have not seen the thing imagined (God). If imagination is all we have, then it's probably the best answer. Another theistic answer is to point out that if we all project our hopes and aspirations onto the canvas of the metaphysical realm, aren't atheists just positing their own patricidal fever dream when they assert the death of God? A case of the kettle calling the pot black? Perhaps. But not everyone who takes up these ideas is necessarily doing it for the same reasons. Some of us arrive at the death of God kicking and screaming. Some of us wept at the grave of God. These sorts of arguments can go around and around endlessly and provide everyone involved with a great deal of food for thought and maybe even some publishing opportunities.

> "Don't you realize that you only believe because you are biased?"
> "OK, but everyone is biased, so you are biased, too!"
> "No, but at least I'm aware of my biases."
> "Oh, but are you really? How do you know? How can anyone know?"

The gist of this kind of dialog seems to be that since the other person has biases, you can safely ignore their claims and happily maintain your own. Sloppy deductive reasoning gives an assist by assuring us that whatever doesn't explicitly disprove our position leaves sufficient wiggle room to maintain our mental status quo. Whatever doesn't kill my argument makes it stronger. How can we break out of this futile engagement style? Curiosity helps. Holding on lightly to previous ideological commitments helps. Resisting instinctual responses helps. Intellectual humility is crucial.

GETTING A PEEK AT THE MAZE

My observation is simply this: All the reasons that people give to defend the truths that underpin evangelicalism turn out to not be such great reasons after all. That's my problem in a nutshell. Miracles are extremely difficult to subject to critical evaluation, and there is to date no clear, documented, supernatural phenomenon that can be observed by everyone and which has no conceivable natural explanation. Personal experience cannot be generalized, it cannot amount to proof, and it can be accounted for by what we already know about the vagaries of the human mind. Historical miracles like the resurrection are even more difficult to evaluate. And philosophical or scientific arguments for the existence of God are difficult; even if they are true, they don't prove enough. There is no reason aside from tradition to give ancient religious sources like the Bible a privileged position. They are just the ideas of ancient people. They can be incredibly insightful on some topics, but that does not prove they are divine by any stretch of the imagination. Humans on their own are capable of insight, creativity, and genius. Ancient religious texts are also full of strange, violent, and naïve claims which modern people are right to reject. And so, it very well may be that God exists and that the supernatural exists. But there isn't any information available to us that clearly shows it. In light of this, conviction-filled demands that we all bow to a so-called revelation "or else" ring hollow and remain unconvincing. The notion that there is something immoral about insisting on evidence sounds like a suspicious circumvention. No one can answer the question, "Why shouldn't I insist on verification?" without appealing to a questionable principle which itself lacks verifiability. All this is to say that, despite all the hoopla, there is no "there" there. It's all smoke and mirrors.

That's my personal view. I don't find any argument sufficiently convincing at this time. It took me years to arrive here, and it shouldn't have. But forces have conspired against me. It feels like I've been navigating a maze all these years, and I finally found a ladder hidden in the vegetation of the maze walls. I climbed hesitantly, fearing I was breaking some fundamental rule, but at the same time thinking *screw the rules*. And the more I climbed, the clearer the paths of the maze became. The maze is not a metaphor for the world, but for the mind's quest for meaning. I'm not suggesting I can see the entire thing, only that when I pay attention to how I think, everything makes just a little more sense. I'm not here because I'm a bad person, or rebellious, or hate God, or refuse to bow to God's plan to my life. It's just the conclusion I've come to after putting some thought into the matter. Could this make me deserving of an eternity of torture by perpetual fire? That outcome seems so incredibly bizarre and unlikely a response to the situation that I would not be able to believe it even if I tried. More likely, it is a last-ditch effort to control me, as if others are grabbing at my heels because they don't want me to climb the ladder and see the maze with greater clarity. Because they like the maze. In fact, they don't think it's a maze. They think the maze is just a path. Never mind that it leads nowhere.

THINGS WHICH ARE SEEN

Theists and supernaturalists might see the "non-disprovability" of God as an opening, and maybe it is. After all, I'm not here saying categorically that God does not exist. But I suggest that the proper religious response to the modern world is humility. That is the best lesson religion can learn from the modern world, if it wants to learn anything new. Knowledge is provisional. Our concept of God must also be provisional. And crucially, faith also ought to be provisional and humble. Intellectual humility is an ethical principle that religion, for all its ethical contributions to humanity's moral treasure chest, has not really keyed into, at least not consistently.

I find it interesting that I have been able to get conservative evangelicals to agree with me about intellectual humility if I pitch it just right. If I say, "God is so vast and incomprehensible. How can we even dare to think that we know anything about him?" Then I get agreement, a thoughtful nodding of the head and a gazing out into empty space as one contemplates the reality of human limitation. But if I try to move the conversation towards humility regarding doctrinal claims, they jump off the bus. In the realm of doctrine there is no room for humility. Doctrine, which is to say basic ideas about the nature of God, is seen as Truth (with a capital "T") and it is not subject to the frailties that are inherent in human thought. But this is a bizarre move. After all, doctrine is held in flawed human minds, and it has manifestly evolved over the centuries. That is a historical fact. Even if one posits that the Bible is the word of God, a perfect guide to life and doctrine in all ways, it must still be understood and believed by people with cognitive biases and cultural and personal predispositions, a situation which would also call for a certain level of intellectual humility. Just because you think the Bible is true doesn't mean you understand it.

This inflexibility regarding the claims of theology and metaphysics is unfortunate because the ideas they embody are still, and perhaps increasingly so, at the root of so many political, social, and personal conflicts in today's world. From suicide bombers driven by absolute convictions who rip apart the bodies of innocent fellow humans, to paranoid interpretations of the political world that lead to violence and social chaos, to campaigns to keep science and reason out of education, to parents shunning their children because of alternate lifestyles the Bible does not approve of. All these things have a lack of intellectual humility at their core: Bringing out the threat of eternal torture to control the thought and behavior of others, applying social and personal pressure against those who think differently, refusing to contemplate proposals that conflict with fixed ideas, claiming a deep commitment to things one barely understands before even attempting to understand them. Again, these things all have one thing in common: lack of intellectual humility. It is bizarre to contemplate the heights of conceit of which the human mind is capable. Whatever your core beliefs about God, religion, or the universe, one thing is undeniable: We are very small and fragile, and we mostly have no idea what we are talking about. Therefore, we ought to speak softly and tentatively about the big ideas that govern our lives.

Intellectual humility is a new thing. It is the gift of science and the enlightenment. It is *the enlightenment* of the human mind. Throughout history we have been accustomed to engaging in epic battles over big ideas. The agreed upon premise of foe and friend alike has always been that only one idea can triumph on this battlefield. But the gift of modern, secular thinking, if you will take it as a gift, is that the triumph of any great idea is a long way off and it can only come about by careful attention to detail and a commitment to objectivity. Therefore, we must be humble and work together over the long haul. Collaboration rather than demonization is the key.

The author of the biblical book of Hebrews famously defines faith as, "being sure of what we hope for and certain of what we do not see" (Hebrews 11:1), and he commends it. But the problem with things which are unseen is that they are also often not there. This is the reason one cannot see them. Do I really need to explain this? The conviction of things unseen led European knights on holy crusades to the Middle East to kill the enemies of God. In the 17th century the same conviction led to the Thirty Years' War, in which two Christian sects, Protestant and Catholic, wrangled over words and control of nations, while, aided by a plague or two, killing roughly a third of the population of Europe. Things unseen led Hitler and his minions to kill six million "evil" Jews. In Stalin's Russia, things unseen led to the death of millions. Stalin himself, guided by things unseen, signed execution orders every night for hundreds of "heretics," and then slept well. Things unseen aided Donald Trump's politics of bullshit; things unseen because they were not there. Things unseen are arguably the most powerful generators of human misery in the world, but things unseen also, in a doubly tragic move, provide comfort to their own victims. It seems we are forever underestimating the power of the human imagination to spin out entire thought structures and interpretive frameworks to impose upon the world, frameworks which have little to no accountability in the realm of hard facts. Most of human history, it seems, is motivated by things unseen. My idea is a simple and perhaps naïve one: Why not focus more on the things right in front of us, which can be seen, and why not demote the things that are unseen just a little bit?

NOTES

1. THE GREAT DIVORCE

1. I'm working here with the idea that the story of the virgin birth was a claim made by Jesus or his contemporaries. Another approach is to ask whether it was entirely fabricated by subsequent Christians, following the well-known pattern in the ancient world of attributing a virgin birth to important figures. For example, the founders of Rome, Romulus and Remus, the Egyptian god Horus, and Ra the sun god.
2. I was predictably very judgmental about my ex-wife's actions for several years, but am much more understanding now. Her journey is just as interesting and valid as mine.

2. THE END ISN'T NEAR

1. All quotations from the Bible come from *The Holy Bible: New International Version* (Zondervan, 1984).

5. THE GOD WHO DOESN'T SHOW UP

1. Italics added for emphasis.
2. Convertedheart, "Rev. F.C. Barnes - If My People (II Chronicles 7:14)," March 12, 2010, YouTube video, 6:25, https://www.youtube.com/watch?v=2S9qZNUASnE. I left in all the spelling and grammar errors of the original.

7. YOU WILL BURN IN HELL FOR THIS

1. For grammatical clarity, I'll note that my daughter uses they/them pronouns.
2. R. H. Charles, ed. *Pseudepigrapha of the Old Testament* (Clarendon Press: 1913), 2:220.

8. THE MESSIAH WHO DOESN'T SHOW UP

1. Exclusions apply. Not valid where prohibited by the Word of God. All allowable miracles must conform to God's mysterious plans. We reserve the right to never disclose said plans. The requester must have sufficient faith. We reserve the right to decide, without any justification or subsequent explanation, whether a purported miracle has been requested with

sufficient faith. We reserve the right to answer a miracle request on the timeline of our choosing, or to not answer it at all for any reason and without any explanation. We reserve the right to answer the miracle request via naturalistic methods which might not appear to be miraculous and might be difficult to identify as such. If you feel that we have not honored the terms of this agreement, you may direct your complaints to God via prayer and they will be answered immediately (see the Prayer Response Terms of Service).

12. CONSCIENTIOUS OBJECTOR

1. I have not been able to source this, so I might have it wrong. But in this context my memory of the quote is more significant than its accurate citation, so I'll leave it at that.

13. TRUTH WITH A CAPITAL "T"

1. C. F. H. Henry, *God, Revelation and Authority* (Crossway Books: 1999), 2:8.
2. I've italicized this section to make it clear that these are my own words, but taking on the persona of my former self as an evangelical.
3. Alvin Plantinga, *Knowledge and Christian Belief* (Grand Rapids: Eerdmans, 2015), x.

14. THE POST TRUTH WORLD

1. Though the term "fascism" or "fascist" is often used as a vague political insult, I am using the dictionary definition: a populist movement that follows an authoritarian strongman who, they perceive, will solve all their problems and resolve their grievances if only given the power to do so.
2. It would appear that these prayers were not answered, at least not by the criteria of those praying.
3. Jeremy Rios, "A Long Erosion in the Same Direction: Trump, Evangelicals, and the Poison of Conspiracy Theories," *Mustard Seed Faith* (blog), December 30, 2020, https://jmichaelrios.wordpress.com/2020/12/30/a-long-erosion-in-the-same-direction-trump-evangelicals-and-the-poison-of-conspiracy-theories.

Printed in Great Britain
by Amazon